THE

NORTHERN EXPOSURE™

C·O·O·K·B·O·O·K

THE

NORTHERN EXPOSURE™
C·O·O·K·B·O·O·K
A COMMUNITY COOKBOOK
FROM THE HEART OF THE ALASKAN RIVIERA

BY ELLIS WEINER
BASED ON THE UNIVERSAL TELEVISION SERIES "NORTHERN EXPOSURE"
CREATED BY JOSHUA BRAND & JOHN FALSEY

CB
CONTEMPORARY BOOKS

Library of Congress Cataloging-in-Publication Data

Weiner, Ellis.
    The Northern exposure cookbook : a community cookbook from the
heart of the Alaskan Riviera / Ellis Weiner : recipes by Barry
Bluestein and Kevin Morrissey.
       p.   cm.
   Includes index.
   ISBN 0-8092-3760-1 (paper)
    1. Cookery.   2. Cookery—Alaska.   3. Northern exposure (Television
program)   I. Bluestein, Barry.   II. Morrissey, Kevin.
III. Northern exposure (Television program)   IV. Title.
TX714.W33   1993
641.5—dc20   93-28636
                                                CIP

All photographs courtesy of CBS.

22   21   20   19   18   17   16   15   14   13   12   11   10   9   8   7   6

To Roslyn and Cicely
with love

🫎 CONTENTS 🫎

4   SOUPS AND STEWS

49

5   ENTREES

59

6   SIDE DISHES

83

🐎 FOREWORD 🐎

I believe it was the Corsican military mastermind—I refer to Napoléon—who said, "An army travels on its stomach." As a matter of fact, it was also Napoléon who coined the phrase "from the sublime to the ridiculous." Both maxims could serve as epigraphs to the volume you now peruse.

In civilian life, as in the military, perseverance begins with food. And when said civilians happen to live here in Cicely, Alaska (pop. 846), the kind of food you run into will span the spectrum from the ineffably sublime to the indescribably ridiculous. I say that, I hasten to add, without condemnation or prejudice. As a person whose culinary talents have won more than a little praise from people of refinement and taste, I know what it takes to learn to cook well—starting with an aptitude I do not hesitate to call innate. Not everyone is born with it, any more than everyone is born with an ability to write an overture like Richard Rodgers or throw a fastball like Nolan Ryan.

Nevertheless, people have to eat three meals a day, and up here in the largest state in the Union, rare is the person who can afford the luxury of having someone else prepare his or her food all the time. That means we've got a lot of people making a lot of meals a lot of ways, ranging from the admittedly gourmet creations of Adam (the man's last name is a mystery, and his personal hygiene strikes me as a bit dubious, but his Cumin Noodles will make you shut

11

your eyes with pleasure) all the way to Marilyn Whirlwind's Seasoned Potatoes (boiled potatoes, salted—serve, eat, and no talking).

Now I have lived in many places; I know that every community has both its gastronomic giants and pygmies, its great regional specialties and its lamentable local disasters. What, then, makes Cicely's collection of culinary favorites worth your while? You'll find the answer in a single word: individualism. Alaska is a great sieve that separates those who want to be left alone to be themselves from the teeming mass of humanity happy to be in close proximity to various voices (individual and institutional) eager to tell them who to be. And the folks of Cicely are as Alaskan as they come.

From Shelly Tambo's Ambrosia Salad to Maggie O'Connell's Gumbo, from Chris Stevens's Glazed Carrots to Ruth-Anne Miller's Pot Roast to my own modest efforts at Chicken-Fried Steak, Poached Salmon, and Pasta with Cayenne Tomato Sauce—what you're holding in your hand is a compendium of recipes from a group of people who have their feet on the ground and their eyes on the future. I take pride in the fact that this is my kind of food, be it sublime or ridiculous, as conceived and executed by my kind of people.

Perhaps it's yours, too. Indeed, perhaps Cicely is your kind of town: for a vacation getaway, a corporate retreat, or an extended communion with nature. Perhaps you're looking to relocate your existing business, or to establish a new one in a congenial locale, or to invest in an area of assured commercial potential in such twenty-first-century industries as tourism, lumber, or mineral extraction. Whatever your need or interest or desire, you'll find your reception here in Cicely, Alaska, as warm as Adam's Warm Duck Salad with Fennel and as bright and sparkling as my own Greens with Balsamic Vinaigrette.

So give Cicely a try. I'll have Holling save you a slice of his Special Lime Chiffon Pie!

Maurice J. Minnifield
Cicely, Alaska
September 1993

☞ INTRODUCTION ☜

This collection of recipes is intended to be sold (God knows where) to raise money to finance the creation of a monument to two women: Cicely, for whom our town is named, and her beloved companion, Roslyn.

They arrived here together at the turn of the century. At that time Cicely didn't even have a name. It did have muddy streets, a wild and rambunctious population of miners and trappers, and a strongman bully named Mace Mowbry, who intimidated absolutely everybody. Roslyn and Cicely drove up in the first automobile to be seen north of Anchorage, took one look around, and decided to turn this squalid little village into a utopian community of artists and free thinkers.

Roslyn was forthright and unshakable, and she could deck a cowboy with a single haymaker. Cicely was delicate and demure and performed interpretive dance. They put

ferns on Main Street and Vienna roast coffee in the bar; they formed a salon and held poetry readings. Together they urged and taught and cajoled and just downright forced those early Cicelians into appreciating culture, themselves, and the life of the mind.

Of course, Mace didn't like that. In the confrontation that ensued, Roslyn spoke on behalf of the town. When one of Mace's men took a potshot at her with a rifle, poor Cicely—who by then was suffering from a serious illness (Dr. Fleischman says it was probably tuberculosis)—threw herself in front of her beloved, taking the bullet instead. The tragic death of this pure and courageous woman had a profound effect on the town. Mace and his boys went straight, and Cicely was named in her honor. As for Roslyn, well, she left and disappeared—but her spirit remained in the town's newfound dignity and humanity. Sooner or later it was inevitable and fitting that somebody decide to commemorate them.

As for who it was, it was Maggie O'Connell. I remember the moment she thought of it. She and Maurice Minnifield were in my store, and for some reason Maurice had got on the subject of a campaign by some man in Texas to erect a monument to the original Mercury astronauts. Naturally Maurice thought that was an excellent idea (and it probably is). But things weren't going so well with the project.

"Can't say I'm surprised," Maurice said. "It's the nature of fame in this society. Fame has become separated from accomplishment. Like a shadow detached from a body. The market gets flooded with these disposable famous people to where there's no room in the public mind for authentic heroes."

Apparently we were supposed to nod sympathetically and share with Maurice a moment of regret at life's unfairness. But if there is one man in North America who has had more than his fair share of fairness, it's Maurice Minnifield, so I just couldn't be bothered. But Maggie looked touched, and said, "That's a shame, Maurice. People who do noble things should be rewarded accordingly."

"Maggie, you know that, and I know that, but try telling it to your average denizen of Oprah and Geraldo." (I wasn't sure he was using "denizen" properly but I kept my mouth shut.) "I mean these people who invoke the word *courage* when they refer to turning down a second helping of chocolate mousse," he went on. "What about the courage it takes to explore the unknown? To brave the terrors of space in order to go up there in a tin can and drop off one of humanity's business cards?"

"You mean like Roslyn and Cicely," Maggie said, though I could see Maurice meant nothing of the sort. "And you're right! There they are, these two women, traveling across the wild territorial frontier, firm in their commitment to each other, and *fearless* in the face of the moral censure and unconcealed disapproval of a chauvinistic male establishment even more barbaric and crude than the one we have to contend with today!"

"Now hold the phone," Maurice said. "You're talking about two women of the . . . *Sapphic persuasion*, remember. What I'm talking about is what Shepard said to me at Schirra's birthday party—"

"I mean, what an accomplishment! To found a town. Think of that, Ruth-Anne."

I agreed it was a wonderful thing, although I remarked that Roslyn and Cicely didn't exactly *found* the town so much as find it and whip it into shape.

"Oh, all right," Maggie said. "But you know what I mean. Our founding mothers. That's who *we* should have a statue for, Maurice."

Well, at that Maurice looked poleaxed. "Those two deviates?"

"Maurice, shame on you!" Maggie said, and proceeded to berate and browbeat him about the merits of displaying a statue to honor Roslyn and Cicely. I kept my mouth shut until Maurice made the mistake of asking my opinion, and I sided with Maggie, pointing out that naming the town for one of the "deviates" hadn't had too bad an effect on it all these years.

"That's because outsiders don't know the history," Maurice said, and he went on and on in that blowhard way of his. He seemed so adamant that I thought the subject was dead, since not much gets done around here without his endorsement. But the idea had put Maggie in one of her inspired moods, and she kept pushing. Pretty much everyone else, it turned out, was in favor of some kind of monument, so a committee was formed and a number of fundraising projects were suggested, including this cookbook. I was prepared to be asked to contribute to it, and I wrote up a few of my favorite recipes. What I *wasn't* prepared for was to be asked to edit it—and to be asked by Maurice!

He popped the question in the store one morning, and I squinted at him for a full minute before my brain worked through all its gears and I figured the whole thing out.

"Maurice, that statue is going to have to be situated somewhere, isn't it? Which means probably in front of the church, or at the bend where Route 1 meets Main Street, or on the front yard of the school. All of which is land you own, if I'm not mistaken. You're going to attempt to sell that land to the committee for a *profit*, aren't you?"

"Ruth-Anne," he chuckled (and I mean *chuckled*). "Nothing worthwhile takes place in this country without somebody making a profit."

Well, in the end, after everyone had submitted their recipes and their commentary, after Maurice himself had gotten emotionally involved in his own contributions—after all that, I held the manuscript hostage. I threatened to burn it, and I think I actually would have done so, had Maurice not signed a legally binding pledge to sell the land to the committee (once the statue was completed and paid for) for the sum of one dollar.

Anyway, here are the recipes. I made no attempt to influence people as to what kinds of dishes they should contribute. This has resulted in occasional duplications of dishes (different versions, of course), but that's kind of interesting in itself. Besides, cooking is a personal thing, and I wanted everybody to contribute the dishes they felt most strongly about. (Plus, they were giving us these recipes for free; when Maurice handed me a list he'd written up called Recipe Recommendations for Contributors, I immediately threw it in the trash and told him we'd take what we were given.) I do offer some brief remarks where it seems appropriate (that's me, talking in italics), and then the contributor introduces the recipe as he or she sees fit. I did rewrite the *directions* of the recipes to make sure they were understandable, and believe me, not all of them were when they were submitted. An unfortunate by-product of this was uniformity of style.

And speaking of unfortunate, I may as well tell you what I had to do with Adam's recipes. It's no secret that he's the best chef in town—when he's in town. But in all other respects he is an extremely difficult person. He refused to write down any of his recipes. But he did consent to *dictate* the ingredients and procedures into a tape recorder. I transcribed these, eliminated all the growling and surliness (most of it, anyway), and edited the remainder. If you can't understand the result, take it up with him.

> Ruth-Anne Miller
> Cicely, Alaska
> September 1993

P.S. Sorry about Maurice's foreword, but since he was giving us the land, I thought I should let him make his little boosterish plug for the town.

P.P.S. Actually, Napoléon said "An army *marches* on its stomach." I looked it up.

1
TODAY'S BREAKFAST SPECIAL

IT'S SIX-FIFTEEN, CHINOOKS. RISE AND SHINE.
I CAN SMELL THOSE GRIDDLE CAKES. MOM'S
SQUEEZING THE VALENCIAS. DAD'S GETTING
READY FOR WORK. TODAY IS FAMILY DAY
HERE ON CHRIS-IN-THE-MORNING.

— CHRIS STEVENS

GRIDDLE CAKES

When Chris Stevens told me this recipe for Griddle Cakes was basically his mother's and not "his," I told him <u>everybody's</u> pancake recipe is their mother's. Later I decided that that was a cozy sentiment, but it wasn't really true.

I know a lot of folks associate griddle cakes with weekend mornings, when Mom or Dad has the leisure to whip up something other than the usual Cheerios or English muffins. My memory is slightly different. Like Proust with his madeleine, the aroma of sizzling flapjacks sends me back to a lost time suffused with emotion. Griddle cakes in the Stevens household meant, not so much that my Mom had the *time* to make them, but that she was actually *home* to make them.

The buttermilk makes a nice sour foil for whatever syrup or honey you pour on top. Makes your coffee seem sweeter, too.

3 cups all-purpose flour
1½ teaspoons baking soda
1 teaspoon salt
1 tablespoon sugar
2 large eggs
¼ cup (½ stick) melted butter
2½ cups buttermilk

"THERE'S A BREAKFAST SPECIAL AT HOLLING'S CAFE TODAY. EGGS BENEDICT, STEAK TARTARE, AND REINDEER SAUSAGE. ALL FOR A MERE $3.95."
— CHRIS-IN-THE-MORNING

1 ♦ Sift flour, baking soda, salt, and sugar together into a bowl. Set aside.

2 ♦ In a large bowl, beat eggs well with a wire whisk. Whisk in melted butter and buttermilk.

3 ♦ Using a wooden spoon, stir flour mixture into egg mixture until smooth.

4 ♦ Preheat an ungreased griddle.

5 ♦ Drop batter by heaping tablespoonfuls onto hot griddle. Cook until bubbles form on the surface of the cakes and edges are firm. Turn cakes and cook for about 2 minutes more on the second side, until lightly browned. Serve hot.

MAKES 4 SERVINGS

ADAM'S GERMAN APPLE PANCAKE

If you haven't done so, you'd better read my Introduction, or what follows will seem even more insane than it probably is.

This is one of Adam's easier recipes—at least it looks fairly easy. Lemon zest, by the way, is cook talk for lemon rind, meaning peel.

Get that thing away from my mouth. The tape recorder. I said *away*, Miller, or I walk. I'm not a politician giving out sound bites.

Yes, the skillet is cast-iron. Do you have a problem with that? Is it too *heavy*? Oh, you don't make eggs in cast-iron? Really? Look, it isn't . . . you . . . you're not frying, all right? You're BAKING. Just get a cast-iron skillet. And remember to dry it immediately after washing. Don't let it DRAIN. Don't—don't ask me *why*. It's obvious *why*. Yes, right: It will *rust*.

Work fast once you melt the butter, because it will burn if you stop to think deeply about your little *life*.

4 large eggs, separated
⅔ cup all-purpose flour
⅔ cup milk
¾ teaspoon salt
1 teaspoon grated lemon zest
1 tart Granny Smith apple, peeled and
    thinly sliced

2 tablespoons sugar
¼ teaspoon ground nutmeg
¼ teaspoon ground cinnamon
3 tablespoons unsalted butter

1 ◆ Preheat oven to 400°F. Place a heavy 10-inch skillet (preferably cast-iron) with an ovenproof handle into the oven.

2 ◆ In a large bowl, whisk egg yolks until well beaten. Add flour, milk, salt, and lemon zest and beat until smooth.

3 ◆ In a separate bowl, beat egg whites with an electric mixer until stiff peaks are formed. Fold into batter. Continue folding until well blended.

4 ◆ In a small bowl, combine apple, sugar, nutmeg, and cinnamon. Stir until apples are thoroughly coated. Set aside.

5 ◆ Remove the heated skillet from oven. Put butter in the skillet and carefully swirl until butter has melted and coated entire surface. Arrange apple slices on bottom of the skillet and pour batter on top. Bake for 8 to 10 minutes, until puffed, firm, and golden. Serve immediately.

MAKES 4 SERVINGS

JOEL ON EATING BREAKFAST

People often ask me how important breakfast is and what it should consist of. (I don't mean people in Cicely. No one here asks me for a scientific overview of anything, with the possible occasional exception of Maurice Minnifield, who more often than not is simply interested in securing some kind of token scientific justification for whatever commercial scheme he happens to be pursuing. Sometimes Ed Chigliak will ask for a scientific opinion about something, and then he'll nod studiously as he totally discounts it, as though he were listening to an aborigine give his religion's explanation for how the universe was created by a snake.)

So, OK, I know what inference could be drawn: people don't think I know what's important. But I don't think that's the case. I would submit that these people don't appreciate the importance of importance. It's a subtle point but I think a valid one.

As for breakfast, some authorities think it should be the biggest meal of the day. Others call for a minimum of twenty grams of protein. My own work in the field has led me to a less doctrinaire position. At this point I believe that breakfast *is* important if you need it to get started in the morning, and the best breakfast is whatever will keep you going until lunch.

THE BRICK'S HOUSE OMELETTE

Holling created this dish, but Dave is the griddle man at The Brick, and since he's made about ten thousand of them by now, I've asked him to introduce this omelette recipe. By the way, as Maurice once said, most canned mushrooms taste more like cans than mushrooms, so it might be better to use them for texture rather than flavor. If you've got fresh mushrooms, so much the better. Sauté them a little, take them out of the pan, and proceed as below.

This is our basic omelette. When Holling hired me he showed me the trick with the pan, how you lift the far edge of the omelette and let the rest of the egg run under and kind of build it up. I remember saying, "Well heck, why don't you just stir everything all together and just cook it down?" But he explained that an omelette is like a package. It's a fluffy thing with a surprise in the middle. So that's how I do it. Not for myself, though. I just stir it up.

3 large eggs
⅛ teaspoon salt
Ground black pepper to taste
2 drops hot sauce (optional)

2 tablespoons butter
¼ cup canned mushroom pieces
½ cup chopped tomato
2 slices American cheese

1 ◆ In a medium-sized bowl, whisk eggs just until blended. Add salt, pepper, and hot sauce (if desired) and whisk until mixed.

2 ◆ Preheat a 7- or 8-inch nonstick skillet over medium heat. Add butter. When it sizzles and foams, pour in eggs, gently shaking the pan to evenly distribute egg across the pan's surface. When egg begins to solidify and curl around the outside, lift the far edge with a fork and tilt the pan downward from the handle toward the far side of the pan, allowing liquid egg in the center of the pan to run down under the set edge. Run the fork around the inside of the pan while swirling the pan to disperse the liquid evenly. Scatter mushrooms and tomato across the top. Cook until omelette sets.

3 ◆ Remove from heat. Place cheese across half the omelette. Using a spatula, fold the other half of the omelette over onto the cheese. Flip out onto a plate.

MAKES 1 SERVING

ADAM'S CURE FOR A HANGOVER

A fresh virgin Mary. Drink it, go home, throw up. You'll feel better.

TODAY'S BREAKFAST SPECIAL

Caribou links, scrambled Eggs, Toast – $2.99
No substitutions, Please.

◆

DENVER OMELETTE

This recipe comes to us from Mrs. Whirlwind by way of her daughter, Marilyn. It's a favorite of mine because ham is packed with flavor and really spruces up what can be a fairly bland affair. It makes me want to say: When in doubt, throw in some ham.

Getting Marilyn to do an introduction was like pulling teeth, but I respect that, in a way.

My mom makes this when we have leftover ham.

Sometimes we fight about it. I say if you make the ham with a glaze, like with honey, it's not as good with anything else as leftovers. Who wants honey with eggs? She says you should make the ham as though you're going to eat it all the first time. She says leftovers are an extra you shouldn't go out of your way to plan for. I think she's living a lie.

4 large eggs	*2 tablespoons butter*
⅛ teaspoon salt	*½ cup cubed cooked ham*
Ground black pepper to taste	*½ cup chopped white onion*
2 drops hot sauce (optional)	*¼ cup chopped green bell pepper*

1 ◆ In a medium-sized bowl, whisk eggs just until blended. Add salt, pepper, and hot sauce (if desired), and whisk until mixed.

2 ◆ Preheat a 7- or 8-inch nonstick skillet over medium heat. Add butter. When it sizzles and foams, add ham, onion, and green pepper. Cook until onion begins to turn translucent (about 5 minutes).

3 ◆ Pour in eggs, gently shaking the pan to evenly distribute egg across the pan's surface. When egg begins to solidify and curl around the outside, lift the far edge with a fork and tilt the pan downward from the handle toward the far side of the pan, allowing liquid egg in the center of the pan to run down under the set edge. Run the fork around the inside of the pan while swirling the pan to disperse the liquid evenly. Cook until omelette sets.

4 ◆ Remove from heat. Using a spatula, fold omelette in half. Flip out onto a plate. Serve with toast.

MAKES 2 SERVINGS

CHRIS'S CURE FOR A HANGOVER

Two raw eggs, Worcestershire sauce, beef bouillon.

Best cure for a hangover is three McDonald's cheeseburgers and a jumbo gulp. But when it's too far to the golden arches, you make do with what you got.

DEVIL'S MESS EGGS

Frankly, I was a little disappointed when Maggie handed me this one. It seems to me that it's just a Denver omelette without the best part (the ham). But Maggie insists the milk makes all the difference. You decide.

Hi! I think it's so great to be able to contribute to this book. Thanks to Ruth-Anne for asking me, and for volunteering to edit it. And thanks to you for buying it, and helping us fund the monument to Roslyn and Cicely.

I'm actually more of a baker than a cook-type cook, but this is one dish I perfected while at college. It's a "devil's mess" because you sort of wreck everything—it's more like scrambled eggs but in the shape of an omelette.

My former—well, *late*, really—boyfriend Rick used to love this. Except for the green peppers, which he just refused to eat. Some love! Then, when he (sort of) came back as a dog . . .

Skip it. But the dog didn't like the peppers, either. Anyway, never mind. You had to be there. But keep the peppers!

8 large eggs
3 tablespoons milk
⅛ teaspoon freshly ground black pepper
¼ teaspoon salt

¼ cup (½ stick) unsalted butter
¾ cup chopped green bell pepper
⅓ cup chopped yellow onion

1 ◆ Put eggs, milk, pepper, and salt into a large bowl. Set aside.

2 ◆ In a heavy frying pan, melt butter over medium heat. Add bell pepper and onion and cook, stirring until onion becomes translucent (about 5 minutes).

3 ◆ Whisk egg mixture. While continuing to whisk, pour mixture into the frying pan. Reduce heat to low and stir gently. Cook to desired consistency, remove immediately from heat, and serve.

MAKES 4 SERVINGS

SHELLY ON ONE-EYED JACKS

Some people like these kinds of novelty foods, you know? Like for breakfast we get a lot of orders for One-Eyed Jacks. That's a piece of toast with a hole in the middle with an egg under it, so the yolk is sticking through the hole. It's supposed to look like an eye, that's how it got its name. And then you melt cheese on the top, that's where the "Jack" part comes in. Of course you could ask for American cheese . . . but a One-Eyed American doesn't sound too delicious, *I* don't think.

ADAM'S EGGS FLORENTINE

I hate to say it, but this is superb. You can get bad Gruyère cheese at a supermarket or better at a specialty store. Either way, this recipe is worth the trouble to make.

I'm not going to waste my time explaining this to you, so as far as you're concerned, Florentine means spinach. Don't ask me why. And please don't *scramble* the eggs. If you can't stand the thought of whole eggs baking like this, then MAKE SOMETHING ELSE.

I created this when I was in Lausanne, Switzerland, waiting for my wife to complete a course of yak-pancreas-extract therapy. OF COURSE THE THERAPY DIDN'T WORK. THE WOMAN'S SYMPTOMS WERE IMAGINARY. Never mind. Just grate the cheese coarsely; you're baking, you can use the texture. Be sure to wash the spinach well and take the time to trim the stems. What? A pinch of nutmeg? No. No. No. NO. Why do you think there's Gruyère? As a GARNISH?

1 pound fresh spinach, washed but not
*   dried, stems removed*
2 tablespoons unsalted butter
½ cup grated Gruyère cheese
8 large eggs
Salt and freshly ground black pepper to
*   taste*

1 ♦ Preheat oven to 325°F.

2 ♦ Put damp spinach into a nonstick frying pan. Cover and cook over low heat until wilted (about 4 minutes). Transfer to a colander and drain.

3 ♦ Put butter into an 8-inch square baking dish and place it in the oven until butter melts. Swirl the pan to coat the bottom and sides.

4 ♦ Squeeze excess water from spinach, chop, and layer evenly on bottom of the baking dish. Sprinkle with 2 tablespoons of the cheese. Carefully crack eggs open over cheese and chopped spinach, keeping the yolks intact. Top eggs with the remaining cheese. Cover tightly with aluminum foil and bake for 12 minutes.

MAKES 4 SERVINGS

CHRIS ON CULTURAL HABITUATION

Once when Holling had a few things to work out on his own, he absconded with The Brick's entire supply of potatoes. Turned out he was putting them to good use: as mash for his still. Talk about trickle-down—that firewater was ten thousand proof. Anyway, that day provided a lesson in cultural habituation. I ordered the special, but instead of home fries with my reindeer patties and scrambled eggs, I found myself looking at a pile of rice. Rice for breakfast? See, I'm used to seeing hash browns, ergo, I see rice, I withdraw. But in India, in China, rice with the morning meal is common practice. So why not? I decided. Besides, take that rice, blast it and toast it and frizzle it up, and you get the second-most American breakfast there is: Rice Krispies.

CHEESE BLINTZES WITH BLUEBERRY SAUCE

Now admittedly, this is a production. But each stage is fairly straightforward, and the result is damned impressive. Note that you cook only one side of the blintze—and you fill it with the cooked side __in__. Isn't that Adam clever.

Don't tell me "it has a lot of steps," Miller. It's the most basic crepe recipe on earth—all right, blintzes, crepes, just shut up and watch. I tried teaching this to the inexpressibly moronic Dave—he treated them like *pancakes*. Do you know how I feel when I stand in that kitchen? You know what *kitchen*, the kitchen at The Brick. I feel like Martin Sheen in *Apocalypse Now*. I want to call in an air strike. "Take out this place NOW. Don't worry about whether I'm here or not. Just do it. Blast this sinkhole of corruption and destroy its EVIL." Ricotta would work, too.

CREPES
¾ cup all-purpose flour
½ teaspoon salt
2 large eggs
1 cup milk
2 tablespoons unsalted butter, melted
2 tablespoons all-purpose flour, if needed
½ cup (1 stick) unsalted butter, at room
    temperature

FILLING
2 cups (1 pound) dry cottage cheese
Yolk of 1 large egg
1 tablespoon unsalted butter, melted
1 tablespoon granulated sugar
½ teaspoon vanilla extract

BLUEBERRY SAUCE
2 cups blueberries (fresh or unsweetened
    frozen, thawed)
2 tablespoons water
1 tablespoon freshly squeezed lemon juice
1 tablespoon confectioners' sugar

1 ♦ Make the crepe batter: sift flour and salt together into a bowl.

2 ♦ In a large bowl, beat eggs with an electric mixer. Add milk and 2 tablespoons of melted butter, beating until well mixed. Add flour mixture and continue to beat until smooth. Cover and refrigerate for at least 30 minutes.

3 ♦ Prepare the filling: combine cottage cheese, egg yolk, 1 tablespoon melted butter, granulated sugar, and vanilla extract. Beat with an electric mixer until smooth. Cover and refrigerate until ready to use.

4 ♦ Make the sauce: puree blueberries, water, lemon juice, and confectioners' sugar in a food processor or blender. Cover and set aside.

5 ♦ Preheat oven to its lowest setting.

6 ♦ Remove crepe batter from the refrigerator. It should be the consistency of heavy cream. If too thin, add up to 2 additional tablespoons of flour to thicken.

7 ♦ Melt 1 teaspoon of the butter in a 7-inch crepe pan or skillet over medium heat, swirling the pan to coat the whole surface. Put 1½ tablespoons of batter into the pan, swirling quickly to spread batter evenly over bottom of pan. Cook until air bubbles begin to form on top and the edges start to curl away from the sides of the pan. Remove crepe with a spatula and flip over, browned side up, onto a plate. Repeat process until batter is used up, melting 1 teaspoon butter in the pan before adding each 1½ tablespoons of fresh batter.

8 ♦ To make a blintze, take a crepe, browned side up, and place 1 tablespoon of filling in the center. Lift the far edge of the crepe up and over the filling, then lift up the near edge, overlapping and crimping the edges together to close. Fold sides up, again overlapping and crimping to secure. Transfer to a plate, and repeat the process with remaining crepes.

9 ♦ Melt the remaining butter in a large frying pan over medium heat. Add a few filled blintzes, seam side down, and sauté until golden brown. Gently turn blintzes over and cook until the other side is golden brown. Remove blintzes from the pan and place on an ovenproof plate. Keep cooked blintzes warm in a very low oven as you sauté the rest.

10 ♦ To serve, place 2 tablespoons of blueberry sauce on the bottom of each serving plate. Place 3 or 4 hot blintzes on top, and dust with confectioners' sugar.

MAKES 16–18 BLINTZES

MARILYN'S CURE FOR A HANGOVER

Hair of the dog.

BISCUITS AND GRAVY

Holling Vincouer says that when he was served this dish, it came with roasted squirrel on the side. We agree that the squirrel is optional.

This recipe for sausage biscuits is adapted from my memory of a meal prepared for Maurice Minnifield and me by the wife of a late friend of ours. The circumstances were less than ideal. We had come to bury her husband, actually.

As for the gravy, which is hers also, it's your basic white sauce with the addition of sausage drippings. Spice it up if you want to, put something green on the side—melon, salad, green beans, or the like—and you're in business for breakfast, lunch, or dinner.

BISCUITS
2 cups bulk breakfast sausage
2 cups all-purpose flour
1 tablespoon baking powder
½ teaspoon salt
2 large eggs, beaten
¾ cup whipping cream

GRAVY
¼ cup all-purpose flour
2 cups milk
¼ teaspoon salt
Freshly ground black pepper to taste

1 ♦ Preheat oven to 400°F. Lightly grease a cookie sheet.

2 ♦ In a heavy frying pan, cook sausage over medium heat until it just begins to brown, breaking it up with a fork. Using a slotted spoon, transfer sausage to paper towels and drain. Remove the frying pan from heat and allow drippings to cool.

3 ♦ Combine 2 cups flour, baking powder, and ½ teaspoon salt and sift into a mixing bowl. Crumble in cooked, drained sausage and mix until sausage is well coated.

4 ♦ In a separate bowl, combine eggs and cream. Add all at once to flour mixture, stirring just enough to moisten dry ingredients. Do not overmix.

5 ♦ Drop batter by heaping tablespoonfuls, about 2 inches apart, onto the prepared cookie sheet. Bake until golden (about 15 minutes).

6 ◆ As biscuits bake, make the gravy. Pour sausage drippings into a large measuring cup and then back into the pan through a strainer. Over low heat, add ¼ cup flour and mix in with a fork until smooth. Continue to cook and stir until mixture browns. While stirring, gradually add milk, ¼ teaspoon salt, and pepper. Continue to cook, stirring constantly, until gravy is smooth, thick, and bubbly.

7 ◆ Place 2 hot biscuits on individual plates and top with hot gravy.

MAKES 12–16 BISCUITS

MAURICE ON WHY HE ISN'T IN THIS SECTION

When I asked Ruth-Anne Miller to edit this volume, I anticipated a certain amount of rivalry and tension between her and myself. It all harks back to when she exercised the option on the mortgage she had with me on her store and bought the establishment for cash. I admit that, at the time, I behaved somewhat vindictively. But I apologized to her, and I was under the impression that she accepted said apology.

Now it turns out that, for no apparent reason, she has seen fit to cut from this book my absolutely top-quality, first-rate recipe for Maurice's Eggs Benedict. She'll probably say it was for space considerations, but I'm a man who recognizes payback when he sees it. In fact, I respect a certain amount of give and take. But in this case, in the context of this charitable project, her omission of my recipe is spiteful and high-handed. She'll deny it, but it is.

[Editor's Note: No, it isn't. Maurice's recipe was omitted due to space considerations. It should be noted that when I asked Maggie O'Connell whether to include it or not, she agreed with me. Other recipes were more appropriate, she said, and added that, in her opinion, eggs Benedict was "the rich man's Egg McMuffin."]

🫎 2 🫎
APPETIZERS

APPETIZERS ARE SUPPOSED TO PERK UP YOUR APPETITE SO YOU GET HUNGRY FOR WHAT COMES NEXT. SORT OF LIKE THE COMING ATTRACTIONS BEFORE A MOVIE. BUT IF THEY'RE GOOD, I END UP EATING THEM, AND THEN I WISH I HAD MORE OF <u>THEM</u> INSTEAD OF THE FEATURE PRESENTATION. IF THEY'RE NOT GOOD, IT SORT OF MAKES ME LOSE MY APPETITE FOR WHATEVER I'M SUPPOSED TO BE SITTING THERE FOR. SO I DON'T REALLY UNDERSTAND APPETIZERS, WHICH IS STRANGE, BECAUSE THEY'RE MY FAVORITE THING. MAYBE I'M NOT EATING THEM RIGHT.
— ED CHIGLIAK

ADAM'S WALNUT TOAST WITH WARM GOAT CHEESE

I asked Adam how something this rich and sweet could qualify as an appetizer. I'll spare you his reply.

I don't expect you to make the bread properly. I don't expect you to have fresh thyme. I don't expect you to do the right thing, which is prepare your own bread crumbs from day-old French bread. I don't expect you to use fresh, unshelled walnuts instead of those prechopped bag-wrapped objects.

All I ask is that once you put the bread and cheese under the broiler, you watch it with undistracted concentration, so that the cheese doesn't run or burn. If you can't do that much, then do me a favor. Make something else. Better yet, stick your head in the oven and keep broiling. Are you still with me, Miller?

WALNUT BREAD
1 tablespoon unsalted butter
2 cups all-purpose flour
2 teaspoons baking powder
1 teaspoon salt
1 large egg
¾ cup milk
¼ cup pure maple syrup
2 tablespoons unsalted butter, melted
¾ cup chopped walnuts

CHEESE TOPPING
1 cup bread crumbs
1 tablespoon chopped fresh thyme or
*   1 teaspoon dried thyme*
1 8-ounce log goat cheese

1 ♦ Preheat oven to 350°F. Grease a 9¼-inch loaf pan with 1 tablespoon butter.

2 ♦ Mix flour, baking powder, and salt together in a large bowl. Add egg, milk, maple syrup, and butter and mix until thoroughly blended. Stir in walnuts. Pour batter into the prepared loaf pan.

3 ♦ Bake for 45 to 50 minutes, until loaf begins to separate from the edges of the pan and a toothpick inserted into center of loaf comes out clean. Remove loaf from the pan and let cool.

4 ♦ Turn the oven up all the way to preheat the broiler. Line a cookie sheet with aluminum foil and set aside.

5 ♦ In a shallow bowl, mix bread crumbs and thyme well. Slice goat cheese into 6 equal rounds. Thoroughly coat each round with bread crumb mixture and place on the prepared cookie sheet.

6 ♦ Cut 6 ½-inch-thick slices of the walnut bread. Place alongside the cheese rounds on the cookie sheet. Place the cookie sheet under the broiler for a few minutes, watching closely, until bread crumbs on cheese rounds are golden brown and walnut bread has toasted.

7 ♦ Put a slice of walnut toast on each serving plate and top with a toasted round of goat cheese.

HOLLING ON THE BRICK

It's like driving a car, really. At first you can't imagine how you're going to get all those different things going at the same time. But pretty soon you learn what *not* to do—what things will take care of themselves while you're taking care of other things. We have a set menu that most people order from. Once that's covered, we can try some specials or experiment with new dishes.

At least I assume that's what I'm supposed to say for a book like this. The truth is, I hardly ever experiment with new dishes. Good Lord, I've been doing this for upwards of twenty years, and I am not a sophisticated person. With our three-man operation (Shelly on tables, Dave on the grill, me on the bar and gadding about), it's all we can do to make the machine work normally, never mind "experimenting with new dishes."

Besides, this is Cicely. Folks who want to eat experiments can go to Sleetmute.

DIEGO'S MAIZ AZUL SUPREME

This is a controversial dish. Frankly, who (besides Adam) has their own tortilla press? But whenever I mentioned the recipe to people around town, they stopped and swooned and their mouths dropped open. Here's Adam to explain its background.

Diego was a colleague, a brother—never mind. Let's just say a friend. We were in Peru, outskirts of Lima—forget "why," forget which agency we were working for IF ANY. "Maíz azul," he would tell me. "Food of the gods." A master with blue corn flour. Give that guy some charcoal briquettes, a few hickory chips, a goat—he could perform miracles. Anyway, he taught me a few things. Until the afternoon he was BLOWN UP in his Deux Chevaux. Those reports that it was a faulty detonator, that the package was to have been delivered to an enemy drop point, delivered by ME, which meant it was ME who should have been in that car, that it should have been MY guts spread out over South America . . . I have no comment. Try me. None.

TORTILLAS
1 cup blue cornmeal (harina de maíz
    azul)
3 tablespoons warm water
1 teaspoon fresh lime juice
Corn oil sufficient to fill a frying pan ½
    inch deep

FILLING
1 avocado
2 teaspoons fresh lemon juice
1 cup shredded red leaf lettuce
1 cup shredded cooked duck breast
1 cup grated Monterey Jack cheese

SALSA
2 cups chopped tomatoes
¼ cup coarsely chopped white onion
2 tablespoons seeded and coarsely chopped
    fresh jalapeño pepper
2 cloves garlic, peeled and finely chopped
1 teaspoon fresh lime juice
2 tablespoons chopped cilantro

1 ◆ Preheat oven to lowest setting.

2 ◆ Make the tortillas: Put cornmeal into a bowl. Add water and lime juice, stirring constantly. Continue to mix until a soft dough is formed. Knead until dough is stiff and no longer sticks to your hands.

3 ♦ Take a sturdy plastic sandwich bag and cut along side seams. Open bag and place half of it on a tortilla press. Break off a small piece of dough and roll between palms to form a ball that is 1 inch in diameter. Place dough ball on the piece of plastic on the press. Fold the other half of the plastic over dough and close the press. Press down until ball is completely flattened.

4 ♦ Remove from the press and cook immediately on an ungreased griddle over medium heat for 2 minutes on each side. Repeat process, cooking each tortilla immediately after it is formed, until dough is used up. Keep cooked tortillas warm in the oven.

5 ♦ Peel avocado, cut in half lengthwise, pit, and slice thin. Toss slices in 2 teaspoons lemon juice and set aside.

6 ♦ Make the salsa: Mix together tomato and onion. Mix in remaining salsa ingredients and set aside.

7 ♦ Make the taco shells: Line a cookie sheet with paper towels and place in the oven. Remove tortillas from the oven. In a heavy, high-sided frying pan, heat about ½ inch of corn oil. Working very fast, slip a tortilla into the hot oil, using a spatula, and fold half the tortilla over onto itself. Insert the spatula between the bottom and top halves of the tortilla to allow oil to circulate and cook for 30 to 45 seconds. Flip tortilla over and repeat.

8 ♦ Remove cooked taco shell from the oil and transfer to the cookie sheet, placing shells on their round ends to drain, resembling rocking horses. Keep cooked shells in the oven as you make the others. Continue process until all taco shells have been made.

9 ♦ Assemble the tacos: Remove shells from oven. Spread a little lettuce across the bottom of each shell. Top with shredded duck meat and an avocado slice. Sprinkle with cheese and spoon on some salsa.

MAKES 12 TACOS

DAVE ON THE BRICK

It's hard work, nice people, OK money. Once a week I get to clean the grease traps and once a month change the air filters, which is like a vacation compared to juggling nine, ten short orders on the lunchtime rush. Every now and then a guy'll pull up front with a caribou or moose he's bagged, and Holling'll make him an offer, and if they make a deal, suddenly I'm in the back with a chain saw carving up legs and steaks. Sure, it *sounds* great, but remember that's kind of rare. Still it beats driving a truck, which I did for sixteen years until I realized: How much radio can you listen to before you go nuts?

ADAM'S POT STICKERS

DOUGH
2 cups all-purpose flour
¼ teaspoon ground cumin
⅔ cup boiling water

FILLING
1 pound ground duck
2 teaspoons finely chopped cilantro
1 teaspoon grated fresh ginger
½ cup (about ¼ pound) chopped raw
    shrimp
½ tablespoon vegetable oil
2 tablespoons soy sauce
2 tablespoons sherry
¼ cup chicken stock or bouillon

1½ tablespoons vegetable oil
⅔ cup chicken stock or bouillon

SAUCE
1 tablespoon grated fresh ginger
2 teaspoons finely sliced scallion
1 clove garlic, peeled and finely chopped
4 tablespoons soy sauce
4 teaspoons rice wine vinegar
¼ teaspoon hot oil
½ teaspoon sugar

1 ♦ Make the dough: Using a fork, combine flour and cumin in a mixing bowl. Slowly add water, stirring constantly with the fork until a soft dough is formed. Cover the bowl with a clean damp cloth and allow to set for 15 to 30 minutes.

2 ♦ Make the filling: Thoroughly mix together all filling ingredients and set aside.

3 ♦ Transfer dough to a floured surface. Knead for 3 to 4 minutes, until dough is smooth and elastic. Cut into 4 equal pieces.

4 ♦ Using a floured rolling pin, roll out dough very thin, 1 piece at a time. From each piece, cut out 6 circles, each 3 inches in diameter, using a cookie cutter or glass. Continue rolling and cutting until there are 24 3-inch circles.

5 ♦ Assemble the pot stickers: Place 1 tablespoon filling in the center of each circle. Wet fingertips. Lift 2 opposite edges of the dough, bring them together over filling, and pinch closed. Continue to pinch along the rest of the seam to seal. Pot stickers should resemble an open fan.

6 ♦ Cook the pot stickers: Preheat a large frying pan over medium heat. Pour in vegetable oil and swirl to coat the bottom evenly. Place pot stickers, flat side down, into the pan. Cook for 1 to 2 minutes, pour chicken stock into pan, and tightly cover. Cook for an additional 10 minutes.

7 ♦ Make the sauce: Mix all sauce ingredients together in a small serving bowl.

8 ♦ Remove the cover from the frying pan and continue to cook until all the stock has evaporated and the bottoms of the pot stickers are golden brown. Transfer pot stickers to a serving plate, and serve immediately with sauce on the side.

MAKES 24 POT STICKERS

MAURICE'S SPICY CHICKEN WINGS

An easy but tasty starter from Maurice. Don't forget to refrigerate, which I always do. Forget, I mean. It does seem to make a difference.

In our culture, cooking on the domestic front is traditionally associated with women. (Professionally, of course, gastronomy is the domain of the male of the species, but that's a different matter.) What, then, impelled me, a United States astronaut and self-made man, to take up the cutting knife and slotted spoon?

In a word, necessity. Anyone born with a discriminating palate in this day and age faces a narrow range of options: find someone of skill who will cook for you (this usually takes the form of a wife), acquire sufficient means to purchase a lifetime's worth of professionally made meals, or learn to cook. Having started out in life with modest means and not having had the good fortune to secure a domestic companion of the female persuasion, I pursued the latter.

Now I have acquired wealth. I could afford the services of a full-time live-in chef. Instead, I cook for myself. I suppose I must be hard-wired to remain self-sufficient in the face of prosperity. Not a boast. Just a simple fact.

40 *chicken drumettes*
¾ *cup soy sauce*
⅔ *cup honey*
4 *teaspoons vegetable oil*
3 *tablespoons dry mustard*

1 ◆ Put drumettes into a plastic bag. Mix remaining ingredients together and pour into the bag. Close the bag securely and shake until chicken is well coated. Refrigerate for at least 2 hours.

2 ◆ Preheat oven to 375°F.

3 ◆ Line a baking sheet with aluminum foil and place a rack on top of the baking sheet. Remove chicken from bag and place on the rack. Bake for 30 minutes, until wings are crisp and golden.

MAKES 8–10 SERVINGS

🐄 3 🐄
SALADS

VINEGAR. VINEGAR, VINEGAR, VINEGAR. A
SALAD IS A DELIVERY VEHICLE FOR VINEGAR.
WHAT'S THE DERIVATION? "BITTER WINE?"
WHATEVER. A SALAD WITHOUT VINEGAR IS
CANDY, IT'S AN INSULT.

LEMON JUICE IS JUST FINE. MAYONNAISE
HAS ITS PLACE. BUT VINEGAR IS ESSENTIAL TO
HUMAN LIFE, PSEUDOMEDICALLY SPEAKING.

— JOEL FLEISCHMAN

THE BRICK'S CAESAR SALAD

This has an interesting history, which I don't want to get in the middle of. I'll let Holling tell it.

When I bought the Brick, I had every intention of just sticking with what the previous owners used to prepare by way of the basic menu. But back then Maurice Minnifield and I saw a lot more of each other than we do today, and one evening he watched me making the big case of salad. We were talking about this and that, and suddenly he's handing me a can of anchovies, the bottle of Worcestershire, a couple eggs . . . until finally I asked if he thought it was funny, throwing unhelpful ingredients at me while I was trying to work.

"I thought you were doing a Caesar!" he said. Now at first I thought he meant I was behaving in some high-handed way, like a Roman emperor. Then he explained about the salad. So I let him teach me how it was done, raw eggs and all, and that was what we served that night. Well, the regulars raved—until I told them it was a Caesar salad. Then they decided they hated it. Thought it was too fancy.

I made it the next night, and when they asked me if it was a Caesar salad, I said, "Naw, that was yesterday. This is just a Roman salad." And they raved again. It took fifteen years before I had the courage to admit—on the menu, in print—that the "Roman" salad was a Caesar salad. By then nobody cared, and it's been a staple on the menu (under its own name) ever since. Today, you'll notice, we cook the eggs a little. It doesn't suffer.

So, really, Maurice should be writing this, not me.

Yolks of 2 large eggs
1 tablespoon white wine vinegar
1 tablespoon water
2 tablespoons fresh lemon juice
¼ teaspoon dry mustard
⅛ teaspoon Worcestershire sauce
1 head romaine lettuce
2 cloves garlic, peeled and crushed
3 anchovy fillets
½ cup extra-virgin olive oil
2 cups croutons
½ cup freshly grated Parmesan

1 ♦ In a small saucepan, combine egg yolks, vinegar, water, lemon juice, mustard, and Worcestershire sauce. Cook over very low heat, stirring constantly, until mixture thickens and bubbles around the edges. Remove from heat and allow to cool.

2 ♦ Separating individual leaves from the head of romaine, wash and dry each leaf. Tear lettuce leaves by hand into 2-inch pieces and place in a salad bowl. Set aside.

3 ♦ Transfer cooled egg yolk mixture to a blender or food processor. Add garlic and anchovies. Process until smooth. Pour in olive oil and continue to process until well blended.

4 ♦ Pour dressing over lettuce and toss, making sure that all the lettuce is coated. Add croutons and Parmesan and toss again.

MAKES 4–6 SERVINGS

ADAM ON SALAD DRESSING

It's called "dressing," all right? Not "swaddling," not "suffocating." You dress the ingredients the way you dress yourself: just enough but not too much. To *flatter*. Not to conceal or drown. You're not making an ice cream sundae. WHY do I have to say this? If you don't— never mind. Turn the tape off.

MAURICE'S GREENS WITH BALSAMIC VINAIGRETTE

1 pound fresh spinach leaves
2 bunches arugula
1 green bell pepper, cut into thin strips
1 jalapeño pepper, seeded and finely
    chopped
2 tablespoons finely chopped green onion
¼ cup balsamic vinegar
2 tablespoons Dijon mustard
⅔ cup extra-virgin olive oil
2 teaspoons fresh lemon juice

1 ♦ Wash and dry spinach and arugula. Tear spinach into small pieces and coarsely chop arugula. Toss in a salad bowl with peppers and green onion.

2 ♦ In a small mixing bowl, whisk vinegar into mustard. While continually whisking, slowly pour in oil until incorporated. Whisk in lemon juice.

3 ♦ Pour dressing over greens and toss.

MAKES 4–6 SERVINGS

POTATO SALAD

I have mixed feelings about including hard-boiled eggs in potato salads. It does add a delicate flavor, but it also threatens to mush up the texture of something that otherwise has some bite. But this isn't my recipe. It's Maggie's.

This recipe has some painful associations for me. As a matter of fact, this is what killed Harry, my (well, one of my) former boyfriend(s). But it wasn't my fault and it wasn't the potato salad's fault. Everyone—except Harry, I guess—knows that you can't leave mayonnaise-based salads in the hot sun, and then just dig in as though nothing is amiss. Which is what happened.

We had a town picnic one summer, I made this, the sun shifted until the table was no longer in the shade, and the potato salad *sat there* and simmered. *All day*, in eighty-five degree heat. By sundown it smelled sort of "off." I *told* him, and *other* people told him, not to eat it. I even tried to physically pull the bowl from his hands. But—you know how men are—he acted as if I was trying to emasculate him. (Is this the horrible real truth about men? That everything, even a bowl of potato salad, stands for their manhood? No wonder the world is such a mess.) Anyway, he fought back, yanked the bowl from me, and had a heaping big plateful. That night he got stomach cramps, drank half a bottle of Pepto-Bismol, and never woke up.

I know. It's awful. But the recipe is simple, tasty, and, when used according to directions, nontoxic.

Serve chilled.

It *wasn't* my fault.

2 pounds small red potatoes, washed
⅔ cup mayonnaise
2 tablespoons chopped fresh dill
½ cup chopped red bell pepper
½ cup chopped celery

2 tablespoons finely chopped onion
½ teaspoon freshly ground black pepper
1 teaspoon salt
1 hard-boiled egg, sliced

1 ♦ Boil potatoes until fork-tender (about 30 minutes). Drain, peel, and quarter potatoes. Mix together all remaining ingredients except egg.

2 ♦ In a large bowl, mix warm potato quarters with dressing. Place egg on top as garnish. Chill at least 2 hours before serving.

MAKES 4–6 SERVINGS

MEA CULPA THREE-BEAN SALAD

Another occasion of salad used as a deadly weapon. This is from Chris Stevens.

Back when I did a morning call-in confessional show, a lady checked in with a tale of remorse about having served three-bean salad the night before to guests. Seems the kidney beans smelled a little funny coming out of the can. Still, she didn't want to waste them . . . in the end, some guests took ill, but, on the up side, no one actually died. She agreed to give me the recipe only if I promised to stipulate that *all* beans (especially of the canned variety) *must be edible, untainted, unspoiled,* and *otherwise wholesome.*

By the way, I've made this dish, and, while I'm personally not much on three-bean salad, it's just fine. Serve chilled, which applies to the cook as well as the salad—i.e., relax and enjoy.

2 cups cooked red kidney beans
1½ cups cooked cut green beans
1½ cups cooked cut wax beans
½ cup thinly sliced white onion
1 red bell pepper, thinly sliced
2 cloves garlic, peeled and finely chopped
¼ teaspoon dry mustard
¼ cup red wine vinegar
1 tablespoon fresh lemon juice
½ teaspoon salt
½ cup vegetable oil
¼ teaspoon freshly ground black pepper
1 tablespoon sugar (optional)

1 ◆ Combine beans, onion, and bell pepper in a large serving bowl. Toss until well mixed.

2 ◆ In a small bowl, whisk together garlic, mustard, vinegar, lemon juice, and salt. While continuing to whisk slowly, add oil. Whisk in pepper and sugar if desired. Pour over bean mixture.

3 ◆ Refrigerate at least 2 hours before serving.

MAKES 6–8 SERVINGS

MAURICE'S COLESLAW

4 cups shredded red cabbage
1 tart Granny Smith apple, cubed
2 tablespoons fresh lemon juice
¼ cup sliced black olives
1 cup chopped celery
¼ cup chopped white onion
1 teaspoon caraway seeds
⅔ cup mayonnaise
½ teaspoon salt
2 tablespoons chopped fresh parsley

1 ◆ In a large serving bowl, toss cabbage with all other ingredients except parsley until mixed thoroughly.

2 ◆ Refrigerate at least 30 minutes to chill. Garnish with parsley before serving.

MAKES 6-8 SERVINGS

WARM DUCK SALAD WITH FENNEL

What many people don't realize is, half the trick of exotic cooking is getting to where the ingredients are, buying them, and bringing them back home. A case in point is this selection from Adam, which (once you've got the duck) could not be easier.

When I mentioned this notion to Adam, of course, he just looked at me with that expression of infinite disgust he has and shook his head. Then he went into one of his sulks. So there are no comments from him regarding this. But frankly, none are necessary.

½ cup orange juice
½ cup honey
½ cup water
1 tablespoon sesame oil
2 teaspoons finely minced fresh ginger
1 teaspoon finely chopped garlic
2 duck breasts, butterflied
2 cups assorted salad greens cut into bite-
    sized pieces
2 tablespoons champagne vinegar
2 tablespoons grated Parmesan
½ cup virgin olive oil
2 fennel bulbs, trimmed and sliced

1 ♦ In a shallow bowl, combine orange juice, honey, water, sesame oil, ginger, and garlic. Mix well. Add duck and let marinate for 30 minutes at room temperature.

2 ♦ Preheat grill or broiler.

3 ♦ Divide salad greens among four plates.

4 ♦ For dressing, combine champagne vinegar, Parmesan, and ¼ cup of the olive oil. Whisk together and set aside.

5 ♦ Using a pastry brush, coat fennel slices with the remaining ¼ cup olive oil.

6 ♦ Remove duck from marinade. Place duck and fennel directly on grill or in a broiling pan and cook for about 5 minutes per side, until duck is browned. Discard marinade.

7 ♦ Place grilled fennel atop salad greens. Slice grilled duck thinly and place on top of greens and fennel. Pour dressing over all. Serve immediately.

MAKES 4 SERVINGS

CHRIS ON CONFESSION

Random thoughts regarding bean salad: That lady who phoned me about the questionable bean salad, I gave her a few words of consolation—something along the lines of, when you eat out, you take your chances. Was that enough? Probably, *these* days, it was *more* than enough. In our hyperindividualistic society, there are very few sources of authority with sufficient legitimacy to really *forgive* you for anything. (Religious orthodoxies excepted, natch.) And yet, there's no shortage of confessing. Check out the talk shows, the tabloid news. Everybody and his estranged, abused, alcoholic adult child of an alcoholic, childish adult brother is on a rampage of telling the world what they did, to whom, with what, and why they might even do it again.

So why, if there's nobody credible to say, "I forgive you," do we confess? To break the karmic logjam of guilt. And once you do, you're allowed to take yourself off the hook. You're no longer "in denial." You're doing "the work." *You're allowed to forgive yourself.* Confession IS absolution. Again: hyperindividualistic. Because who better to absolve you than yourself?

Like the song says, "Don't go to strangers, darling."

SHELLY'S AMBROSIA SALAD

I think it's admirable when people make a sincere effort to do something they may not be entirely suited for, when it's for a good cause.

Holling says folks at The Brick scarf this big time, so here it is. Not everybody is a coconut person, but if you are, go for it.

1 11-ounce can whole segment Mandarin oranges, drained (liquid reserved)
1 cup flaked coconut
¼ cup sliced maraschino cherries
1¼ cups miniature marshmallows
1 cup whipped cream

1 ♦ In a large bowl, mix together orange segments, coconut, cherries, and marshmallows.

2 ♦ In a separate bowl, mix together reserved orange liquid and whipped cream.

3 ♦ Fold whipped cream mixture into fruit. Cover and chill for at least 1 hour.

MAKES 6 SERVINGS

4

SOUPS AND STEWS

WHY IS AMERICA CALLED A MELTING POT AND NOT A STEW POT? MAYBE BECAUSE WOMEN MAKE DINNER IN THE STEW POT, BUT MEN BREW ALLOYS IN THE MELTING POT, AND LABELING SOCIETY IS—FOR BETTER OR FOR WORSE—TRADITIONALLY A MAN'S GAME. OF COURSE, YOU LOOK AROUND, THE MELTING POT'S IN DISREPUTE, OBSOLETE. IT'S DISRESPECTFUL OF CULTURAL DIFFERENCES, IT'S CHAUVINISTIC, IT'S DISENFRANCHISING TO MINORITIES. WHAT IS THERE LEFT TO BELIEVE IN?

THE ETERNAL VERITIES OF A NICE HOT BOWL OF STEW.

— CHRIS STEVENS

BUBBE FLEISCHMAN'S CHICKEN SOUP

I think I read somewhere that chicken soup really is good for a cold. But if you have a cold, the last thing you'll feel up to doing is standing over a stove cooking. So you might want to either make it ahead of time and freeze it, or get someone else to make it for you.

This particular chicken soup recipe is courtesy of Joel, who got it from his grandmother.

This is the standard item I have eaten since birth at Seders and other family gatherings. Its virtue is its purity. I once asked Bubbe if she had any scallions I could throw in. (There's virtue in purity, sure, but let's face it—virtue has never been big on flavor.) She saw me coming a mile away. "What, you want it should be wonton soup?" she said. "So go to a Chinese."

"But it's kind of . . . bland," I said.

"Jews don't eat scallions," she replied.

And they don't, at least not in chicken soup. Unfortunately, apparently, they do eat parsnips. Good luck.

1 4–5 pound frying chicken, cut in half
1 whole yellow onion, peeled
3 carrots, trimmed and cut in half
1 bay leaf
1 parsnip, trimmed and cut in half
3 celery ribs, with leaves
12 cups water
1 tablespoon salt

1 ♦ Put all ingredients into a large stockpot. Bring to a rapid boil over high heat. As soon as water boils, turn heat down to low and simmer. Skim off the foamy residue that will form on the top after a few minutes. Continue to simmer, uncovered, for about 3 hours, until chicken falls off the bone when speared with a fork, skimming top of soup whenever necessary.

2 ♦ Transfer chicken to a platter and refrigerate. Discard all other solid ingredients and strain stock into a large bowl. Refrigerate stock, uncovered, for at least 2 hours. (If refrigerating overnight, cover after 3 hours.)

3 ♦ Once chicken has cooled, remove skin and meat from the bone. Shred meat and refrigerate until ready to proceed with the stock. Discard skin and bones.

4 ◆ Remove stock and shredded chicken from the refrigerator. Using a large spoon, skim off and discard fat that has congealed on surface of stock. Combine stock and chicken in a large pot and cook over medium heat for about 15 minutes, until thoroughly heated.

MAKES 8–12 SERVINGS

MARILYN'S FRESH TURNIP SOUP

If turnips make you nervous, you're not alone. But don't worry. This creamy soup, from Marilyn's mother, is basically a puree; you could serve it to a child.

My mom makes this when there are turnips at the market. Sometimes, if I'm home when she's cooking, I ask her if she wants me to help. She says no, she doesn't really need any help. Then she says, Unless I really want to. And I say no.

2 cups peeled and chopped turnips
½ cup peeled and chopped small red
*   potatoes*
4 cups homemade chicken stock or canned
*   chicken broth*
1 cup milk
⅛ teaspoon white pepper
¼ teaspoon salt
¼ teaspoon ground nutmeg

> **"AS WE CICELIANS LIKE TO SAY . . . IF IT'S NOT SOUP, IT'S WET BREAD!"**
> **— ED CHIGLIAK**

1 ◆ Combine turnips, potatoes, and stock in a medium-sized saucepan. Cook over medium heat for about 20 minutes, until vegetables are fork-tender. Remove from heat.

2 ◆ Transfer entire contents of the pan, including liquid, to a food processor or blender and puree to a smooth consistency. Return mixture to the saucepan and bring to a boil over medium heat. Boil 2 minutes. Remove from heat, whisk in remaining ingredients, lower heat, and cook just until soup begins to steam (*do not bring back to a boil*). Serve with Marilyn's Seasoned Potatoes (see Index).

MAKES 6–8 SERVINGS

ADAM'S LAMB STEW

Another opera production from you-know-who but, like all the others, worth it.

Give me that pan. For the onions, all right? Does that meet with your approval? No, no, you DON'T put them in with the lamb. *Because.* Because they're small, they'll stew up and break down and turn to mush. A stew is a symphony, Miller, hasn't anyone ever told you that? Which does not mean "smear everything together and hope for the best." It means discipline and balance.

What? Where did I get this recipe? It's LAMB STEW, Miller, where do you think I got it? I got it from the proprietor of a public house near a quiet little village in county Sligo on a fanciful ramble through the auld sod. I got it from the cantankerous wife of a butcher in a tiny town in rural Provence. I got it off the side panel of a box of Wheaties. It's none of your business where I *got* it.

¼ *pound uncooked sliced bacon, cut into thin strips*

3 *pounds lean lamb stew meat (usually a combination of shoulder, breast, and neck), cut into 2-inch cubes*

2 *teaspoons olive oil, if needed*

1 *carrot, peeled, trimmed, and sliced in rounds*

1 *white onion, peeled, cut in half, and sliced with the flat side down*

1 *leek, white and light green parts only, cut in half lengthwise, rinsed thoroughly between each layer, and sliced*

3 *tablespoons all-purpose flour*

1 *bay leaf*

¼ *teaspoon white pepper*

2 *teaspoons chopped fresh thyme or ¾ teaspoon dried thyme*

2 *large cloves garlic, peeled and finely chopped*

1 *bottle good-quality red wine, Beaujolais, Chianti, or Bordeaux*

¼ *cup (½ stick) unsalted butter*

24 *whole small white onions, peeled and trimmed*

¼ *cup beef broth*

24 *white button mushrooms, cleaned and trimmed*

½ *cup chopped fresh parsley*

1 ♦ Preheat oven to 350°F.

2 ♦ In a 4-quart enamel French oven (oval Dutch oven), sauté bacon over medium heat until lightly browned (5 to 6 minutes). Using a slotted spoon, transfer bacon to a large bowl.

3 ♦ Brown lamb in the bacon fat, a few pieces at a time. As lamb is cooked, add it to the bacon in the bowl.

4 ♦ Add olive oil to the French oven if needed (if insufficient bacon fat remains for browning the vegetables). Add carrot, onion, and leek. Cook, stirring constantly, for about 5 minutes, until vegetables just begin to brown. Remove the pot from heat.

5 ♦ Sprinkle flour over bacon and lamb and toss to coat evenly. Place in the French oven with vegetables. Cook over medium heat, stirring constantly, until the meat forms a light crust (4 to 5 minutes). Pour off any fat that remains in the pot and return the pot to heat.

6 ♦ Add bay leaf, pepper, thyme, and garlic. Stir in wine. Bring to a simmer, cover, and place in the oven. Cook for 2 hours.

7 ♦ After lamb has been in the oven 1½ hours, put 2 tablespoons of the butter into a large pan that has a tight-fitting cover. Melt butter over medium heat. When butter begins to bubble, add onions. Cook for about 10 minutes, shaking the pan every so often so that onions will roll and brown on all sides. Add beef broth. Bring to a boil, cover, reduce heat, and gently simmer for about 20 minutes, until onions are tender.

8 ♦ While onions are simmering, put the remaining 2 tablespoons butter into a large frying pan over medium heat. Once butter has melted, add mushrooms in a single layer and cook for about 15 minutes, until browned, tossing occasionally to ensure even browning.

9 ♦ To serve, ladle equal amounts of lamb stew in the center of six serving plates. Ring with alternating whole onions and mushrooms. Sprinkle with parsley.

MAKES 6 SERVINGS

JOEL ON JEWISH COOKING

Look, let me amplify what I said before about chicken soup. It IS bland. I mean, let's be honest. The point wasn't to insult my grandmother or act out some kind of generational gourmet one-upmanship. But you live in New York, you see it all and eat it all, and believe me, by the age of eight you know that Szechwan double-cooked pork is colorful and tasty—a little sweet, a little spicy—whereas Aunt Rose's brisket had more flavor *before* it was cooked. Plus, all those glutenous Yiddish dishes—kishke, tsimmis, even kugel—what's to like?

When I was a kid, I would blanch and turn away from a passing platter of such stuff. My father, though, would load up his plate with it (let's not even think about the word *cholesterol*; we'll pretend it didn't exist before 1982), dig in, and say to me and my cousins, "You kids don't know what's good. This tastes like candy!"

I distinctly remember thinking, "No. A Zero, a Snickers, a PayDay—THEY taste like 'candy.' This stuff will be lucky if it tastes like food."

So. Does that make me a bad Jew? You decide.

THE BRICK'S KICK-ASS CHILI

Here it is, my favorite. And like most stews, it's even better the next day. So do yourself a favor. Make it yesterday. Right, Holling?

This is an example of what Chris once called a "folk recipe." It's the latest version of a dish that almost every customer who's ever eaten chili in The Brick has voiced an opinion about. The bacon is Maurice's idea. The tomatoes, which are kind of heretical, come from Ed's uncle. The cayenne and chili powder is standard issue, but look at that coriander—that couple that owned the circus Mr. Bellati was traveling with? The lady suggested that.

A year from now this'll probably be different, but right now it seems to do the trick. Serve Tabasco on the side.

6 *slices uncooked thick bacon, cut into cubes*
2 *large yellow onions, peeled and chopped*
1 *tablespoon vegetable oil (if needed)*
5 *pounds lean beef chuck, trimmed and cut into ½-inch cubes*
1 *28-ounce can whole tomatoes*
2½ *cups canned beef broth*
¼ *cup ground cumin*
1 *tablespoon dried oregano*
1 *tablespoon ground coriander*
1 *teaspoon cayenne pepper*
2 *tablespoons chili powder*
1 *teaspoon salt*
4 *cloves garlic, peeled and finely chopped*

> "CHILI CAN BE ALL RIGHT, AS LONG AS THERE AREN'T TOO MANY BEANS IN IT. YOU GET TOO MANY BEANS AND YOU'RE MORE IN THE REALM OF A VEGETABLE SIDE DISH."
> — CHRIS STEVENS

1 ♦ In a large skillet, fry bacon over medium heat for 5 to 6 minutes, until crisp, stirring periodically. Using a slotted spoon, transfer bacon to a large stockpot.

2 ♦ Add onions to the skillet, reduce heat to low, and cook until onions begin to wilt and turn translucent (about 5 minutes). Using a slotted spoon, transfer onions to the stockpot.

3 ♦ Add vegetable oil to the skillet if needed (if there is insufficient bacon fat remaining for browning beef chuck). Sauté beef, a few cubes at a time, until just browned on all sides. As meat is browned, place in the stockpot.

4 ♦ Add tomatoes and their juice to the stockpot. Crush tomatoes slightly with the side of a spoon. Stir in all remaining ingredients.

5 ♦ Raise heat to high and bring to a boil. Skim off any foam or fat that rises to the top. Lower heat and simmer, uncovered, for about 3 hours, until meat is very tender and sauce is thick.

6 ♦ Serve in deep soup bowls, along with saltines.

MAKES 6-8 SERVINGS

CHRIS ON CHILI ADDENDA

Kidney beans. Cheddar cheese. Monterey Jack shreds. Cilantro. Sour cream. Chopped onions. Chopped scallions. Macaroni. Parsley.

There's something about chili that makes me want to be orthodox. Even cilantro, which is my favorite herb, seems like a gate-crasher at the mansion of chili con carne. A matter of one palate's arbitrary preference? No way—all those add-ons taste just fine with the basic bowl of red. So what is it that makes me shun all garnish and eschew optional toppings?

Call it a desire to enjoy something basic. Better yet, call it a desire to be reminded that something basic can still exist. Love comes and goes, leaving you to take it on faith that it was ever really there. Philosophy, like the man said, doesn't so much solve problems as abandon them. Sex makes you believe intensely things you know you don't believe. Money's a trap, nature is red in tooth and claw, art starts to seem personal . . . yeah, but in a bad way. God? Not at His desk and not expected back anytime soon. All those potential fundamental elements of a good life, all those compass needles and cornerstones . . . pretty soon, each is shot to hell one way or another.

Pass the chili.

MAGGIE'S GUMBO

1 cup (2 sticks) unsalted butter
1 cup peeled, trimmed, and finely chopped
    carrot
1 cup finely chopped white onion
1 cup finely chopped celery
½ cup all-purpose flour
1 cup bottled clam juice
3 cups homemade chicken stock or canned
    chicken broth or water
1 28-ounce can whole tomatoes, drained
    and coarsely chopped

4 bay leaves
2 cups fresh or canned crabmeat, drained
    and picked clean of any filament
2 cups raw shrimp, cleaned
1 pound cracked crab claws
2 cups thinly sliced zucchini rounds
1 teaspoon salt
½ teaspoon white pepper
½ teaspoon ground cumin
⅛ teaspoon cayenne pepper
3 cups cooked white rice

1 ♦ In a heavy 4-quart casserole or Dutch oven, melt butter over medium heat. Add carrot, onion, and celery and sauté until lightly browned (about 10 minutes).

2 ♦ While stirring constantly, add flour and cook for 5 to 6 minutes, until golden brown. Whisk in clam juice and stock. Continue to whisk until smooth. Reduce heat and simmer for 5 minutes.

3 ♦ Add all remaining ingredients except rice. Stir, cover, and simmer for an additional 20 minutes.

4 ♦ Serve over rice.

MAKES 4–6 SERVINGS

ED ON BOWLS

If you were stranded on a desert island, and all you could have would be one thing for eating out of, you'd choose a bowl. The bowl would handle all your appetizers, all your chicken and roast beef and stews and stuff like that, all your vegetables, potatoes, rice, noodles, pasta, ice cream—everything.

Of course, on a desert island, you might not have the opportunity to eat much roast beef or chicken or ice cream. But it would be good to know that, if any showed up, you could.

🐂 5 🐂
ENTREES

I USED TO THINK THEY WERE CALLED ENTREES
BECAUSE IN A RESTAURANT THAT'S HOW THEY
BROUGHT THEM TO YOUR TABLE. ON TRAYS.
NOW I KNOW BETTER.

— SHELLY TAMBO

THE BRICK'S TUNA SUPREME

2 7-ounce cans tuna, drained and flaked
½ cup chopped green onion
½ cup chopped celery
½ cup chopped pimiento-stuffed green
    olives
½ cup chopped green bell pepper
½ teaspoon salt
⅛ teaspoon ground black pepper
⅔ cup mayonnaise
1 teaspoon lemon juice
6 slices wheat bread, toasted
6 slices Swiss cheese

> "BREAKFAST IS THE MEAL OF HOPE. DINNER IS THE MEAL OF REWARD. THAT MAKES LUNCH THE MEAL OF ... I DUNNO ... BUSINESS AS USUAL."
> —CHRIS STEVENS

1 ♦ Preheat broiler.

2 ♦ Combine all ingredients except wheat bread and cheese in a large bowl and mix thoroughly.

3 ♦ Spread equal amounts of tuna mixture on each slice of toast. Top each with a slice of cheese.

4 ♦ Put open-face sandwiches on a cookie sheet lined with aluminum foil and broil for about 5 minutes, until cheese has melted and lightly browned.

MAKES 6 SERVINGS

DAVE'S SALMON STEAKS

Anyone who lives in Alaska gets used to seeing salmon on their plate more often than not, which is just fine with us. Of course, different people have different ideas about how it should be prepared. Here's Dave's, which he serves at The Brick.

I don't understand the comments I get. What are potato chips? Potatoes, oil, and salt. You ever eat potatoes with salmon? You ever eat oil with salmon? You ever eat salt with salmon? So what's the problem? And that crunch is just great.

1 large egg
2 tablespoons milk
½ teaspoon salt
¼ teaspoon sweet paprika
⅛ teaspoon ground black pepper
1¼ cups crushed potato chips
1¼ cups crushed saltines
6 approximately 6-ounce salmon steaks

1 ♦ Preheat broiler. Line a broiling pan with aluminum foil. Lightly grease the foil and set the pan aside.

2 ♦ In a shallow bowl, combine egg, milk, and spices. Mix thoroughly.

3 ♦ In a separate shallow bowl, mix together chips and saltines.

4 ♦ Dip each salmon steak into egg mixture and then in the chip-saltine mixture. Coat well.

5 ♦ Put steaks on the broiling pan. Position pan approximately 6 inches from the source of heat. Broil steaks for 6 minutes on each side, until coating is brown and salmon flakes easily.

MAKES 6 SERVINGS

SALMON LOAF

I'm not much on canned salmon, but this recipe is actually quite tasty. Holling says he keeps it on the menu for those times when he's fresh out of fresh, but I think his motives are more sentimental than that.

I suppose you could say this is for when you want salmon when there isn't any salmon. Fresh, I mean. Serve it as is, or slice it cold and have it on some decent bread. I admit it's not as good as Maurice's (or even Dave's), but when they're not biting and you're reduced to the can, you could do worse.

¼ cup (½ stick) unsalted butter
1 white onion, peeled and chopped
1 rib celery, chopped
3 tablespoons chopped fresh dill
¾ cup bread crumbs
2 hard-boiled eggs, chopped
⅔ cup heavy cream
2 tablespoons fresh lemon juice
1 large egg, beaten
1 teaspoon coarse salt
¼ teaspoon freshly ground black pepper
3 7-ounce cans pink salmon, drained,
    rinsed, and flaked

1 ◆ Preheat oven to 375°F.

2 ◆ Melt 2 tablespoons of the butter in a small frying pan. Add onion, celery, and dill and sauté over medium heat until onion begins to brown (about 5 minutes).

3 ◆ Remove pan from heat and transfer vegetables to a large bowl. Add all remaining ingredients except butter and mix thoroughly.

> "YOU KNOW, I CAN STILL REMEMBER EVERY DETAIL OF THE DAY SHELLY CAME TO CICELY. IT WAS TUESDAY. I'D HAD A GOOD LUNCH CROWD — RAN OUT OF THE SALMON LOAF. MAURICE CAME INTO THE BAR AND BEHIND HIM . . . THERE SHE WAS. THE MOST BEAUTIFUL YOUNG LADY I'D EVER SEEN.
>   THERE WAS A KIND OF ELECTRICITY IN THE AIR. MY HEART WAS POUNDING. OF COURSE, I MADE EVERY EFFORT TO HIDE MY FEELINGS, BUT I COULD FEEL HER GAZE. AND FROM THAT MOMENT I WAS A LOST MAN . . . AND THE HAPPIEST MAN ON THE FACE OF THE EARTH."
>   —HOLLING VINCOUER

4 ♦ Transfer mixture to a 9¼-inch loaf pan.

5 ♦ Melt the remaining 2 tablespoons of butter. Brush on top of the loaf.

6 ♦ Bake for 20 minutes, until lightly browned on top.

MAKES 6–8 SERVINGS

MIKE MONROE ON THE GREATEST FOOD IN THE WORLD

About five years ago the food writer for the *Atlantic* published a piece on pasta, which he called "the world's greatest food." He was wrong. Much as I love pasta, I have to say that it's the world's second-greatest food.

The world's first-greatest food has these qualities, all of which leave pasta in the dust: It's a great source of protein. It's very low in fat. It can be served for breakfast, lunch, or as an ingredient with dinner, when it can be used (as marinade or the basis for a sauce) with any kind of meat, fish, or vegetable. It can be served with fruit. When combined with a sweetener, it makes a great dessert; when combined with a little liquid, it makes a great beverage. About the only thing you *can't* serve it with is ice cream—and it makes a good substitute for ice cream.

Its health benefits—to digestion, to bone nourishment—are well known. You can make it yourself. About the worst thing you can say about it is that it requires refrigeration.

The best food in the world (and will someone please show this to Corby Kummer, that *Atlantic* writer?) is yogurt.

I've been waiting five years to get this off my chest. Thanks, Ruth-Anne.

MAURICE'S POACHED SALMON

Some folks have a rather elitist attitude toward cooking. Those folks generally have an elitist attitude about life in general, though, so I suppose it's to be expected. (That's an observation, Maurice, not a personal swipe at you.)

The temptation with salmon is to do too much. I just bring the broth to a boil, simmer it down a bit to concentrate the flavors, then lay in the fish, turn off the heat, and go about my business. The fish poaches herself just right. Add a Napa Valley reserve chardonnay, and you're as close to heaven as you can get without sprouting wings.

14 cups water
2 cups dry white wine
2 large white onions, peeled and cut into
　　chunks
2 ribs celery, with leaves, broken in half
12 whole black peppercorns
3 large carrots, peeled, trimmed, and cut
　　into chunks
2 large cloves garlic, peeled and cut in
　　half
6 sprigs fresh dill
3 bay leaves
2 teaspoons salt
1 5-pound whole salmon, cleaned

1 ◆ Combine all ingredients except salmon in a large fish poacher or turkey roaster and bring to a boil over high heat. Lower heat and simmer for 30 minutes.

2 ◆ Put salmon onto the poaching rack or onto a rack that is long enough to support the whole fish and will fit in the roasting pan.

3 ◆ Bring poaching broth to a boil over high heat. Carefully submerge the rack into the boiling broth (with the aid of tongs if you are using a roasting pan rack rather than a fish poacher rack, which has handles). Bring back to a boil. Cover tightly, boil for 1 minute, turn off heat, and allow fish to poach to an internal temperature of 140°F. (This will take at least 30 to 45 minutes.)

MAKES 6–8 SERVINGS

ADAM'S SZECHWAN CHICKEN

This apparently was the first dish Adam prepared for any of us in Cicely. He made it when Joel stumbled on his cabin, because—well, let him tell you in his own charming way.

Because I was HUNGRY, all right? You think I put on a spread for *company*? To be *hospitable*? Or maybe I wanted to show off for this bright young physician! Look, Miller: I had the chicken, it was going to spoil, I cooked it. Dr. Kildare just happened to be there. Next time I'll cook *him* and make tedious small talk with the chicken.

2 ounces dried shiitake mushrooms
½ cup boiling water
¼ cup peanut oil
2 large (about ¾ pound each) whole
    chicken breasts, skinned, boned, and
    julienned
1 red bell pepper, julienned
2 bamboo shoots, julienned
1 teaspoon minced scallion
1 teaspoon finely chopped garlic

2 tablespoons soy sauce
1½ tablespoons rice wine vinegar
1 tablespoon sugar
1 tablespoon dry sherry
½ teaspoon freshly grated ginger
⅛ teaspoon white pepper
2 tablespoons cornstarch
2 tablespoons water
2 teaspoons sesame oil

1 ♦ Combine mushrooms and boiling water. Set aside for 30 minutes.

2 ♦ Heat peanut oil in a wok over medium-high heat. Add chicken and cook about 2 minutes, stirring constantly, until lightly browned. Remove with a slotted spoon and let drain on paper towels.

3 ♦ Drain mushrooms, remove and discard stems, and slice into julienne strips.

4 ♦ Put mushroom strips, bell pepper, bamboo shoots, scallion, and garlic into the wok. Cook for 1 minute, stirring constantly. Add soy sauce, vinegar, sugar, sherry, ginger, and white pepper. Cook for 1 more minute, stirring constantly. Mix in drained chicken.

5 ♦ Combine cornstarch and water in a small bowl. Slowly stir into mixture in the wok, until sauce has thickened. Add sesame oil, mix, and transfer to a serving plate. Serve with rice.

MAKES 4-6 SERVINGS

CHICKEN POT PIES

Don't turn up your nose if this recipe title reminds you of those frozen things in the supermarket. These pot pies are better and not much harder to make—at least that's what Holling tells me.

About ten years ago I had a regular customer who came to The Brick strictly for the society. Can't say as I blame him—he lived alone out in the woods, doing some kind of code-breaking work for the Pentagon. But the thing of it is, he wanted to be served only the kinds of foods he could make or buy for himself. So he might order, say, macaroni and cheese, or cream-filled cupcakes, or peanut butter and jelly sandwiches—you get the idea. One day he asked for a chicken pot pie, and I proceeded to prepare a serving of what he and I agreed was an absolute disaster.

Well, my lady friend at the time—this was before Shelly, of course—told me about frozen pie dough, and while I don't want to say "it changed my life," it sure changed those chicken pot pies.

The customer liked them, too. Finally he was transferred to New Zealand and we never heard from him again. Well, that's not quite true. We did get one postcard, but it looked like it was written in gibberish, and no one could read it.

1½ cups sliced celery
1½ cups peeled, trimmed, and chopped
    carrot
5 cups cubed cooked chicken
1 10-ounce package frozen peas, thawed
1 6-ounce can mushroom slices
4 cups homemade chicken stock or canned
    chicken broth

1 cup milk
½ teaspoon celery salt
¼ teaspoon ground black pepper
¼ teaspoon ground nutmeg
⅔ cup all-purpose flour
¾ cup water
2 flat sheets of ready-made pie dough

1 ♦ Preheat oven to 425°F.

2 ♦ Fill a saucepan with 1 inch of water and bring to a boil over medium heat. Add celery and carrot and cook for 10 minutes. Remove from heat. Transfer to a colander, rinse under cold running water, and drain.

3 ♦ Put celery, carrot, chicken, peas, and mushrooms into a large bowl. Toss together to mix thoroughly. Distribute evenly among six 5-inch round casserole dishes.

4 ♦ Combine stock, milk, celery salt, pepper, and nutmeg in a heavy saucepan and bring to a boil over medium heat. Remove the saucepan from heat.

5 ♦ In a small bowl, mix flour and water to a smooth paste. Stir into the saucepan. While continuing to stir, return pan to medium heat and bring back to a boil. Lower heat and simmer, stirring constantly, for about 2 minutes more, until mixture is thick and smooth. Pour sauce in equal amounts over the chicken-vegetable mixture in the 6 casseroles. Set aside to cool.

6 ♦ Lay a sheet of pie dough on a floured surface. Using a clean 5-inch round casserole dish, cut 3 dough circles from the sheet. Repeat process with second sheet of dough. Lay a dough circle atop each of the individual casseroles, crimping the outer edge of dough down over each dish rim. With a sharp-pointed knife, make 3 small incisions near the center of each crust to allow steam to escape.

7 ♦ Put casseroles on a cookie sheet and bake for 30 minutes, until crust is golden and filling is bubbly.

MAKES 6 SERVINGS

ED ON SURPRISES IN FOOD

In eighth grade I had a science teacher who was pretty boring most of the time. One day he asked us what the purpose of the human mouth was in terms of taking in nourishment. Someone said biting, someone said chewing, someone said swallowing, someone even said starting the digestion process with saliva. Then he said, What else?

No one knew. He let us sit there for about five minutes in silence. It felt like three hours. Finally he said, Selecting. It's the one thing I learned in science that year, and it really hit home last year when I found a ring in a fish I had caught. It was given to Federico Fellini by Giuletta Masina as a present. How did it get into the fish? We'll probably never know. How did I find it and why didn't I swallow it? My mouth selected it.

JOEL'S ROAST GROUSE

Joel shot a grouse on his first hunting trip. He winged it, was overcome with remorse, nursed it along back in his office, and mourned when it died. He also ate it. There's a lesson in that for all of us, but I'm damned if I know what it is.

Look, it's true I'm not the world's best cook, but this recipe is OK. I got it from my Uncle Bernie, who is actually a very competent chef and likes to experiment with game. I don't know—Jews cooking game, Jews shooting game . . . it feels weird. He says you can substitute six Rock Cornish hens for the grouse. Should it be grouses? Grice? Nothing sounds right—which maybe is a sign from God.

½ *cup (1 stick) melted butter*
1½ *cups cooked wild rice*
½ *cup chopped celery*
½ *teaspoon ground thyme*
½ *teaspoon dried marjoram*
3 *cleaned grouse* or 6 *Rock Cornish hens*
3 *tablespoons butter, room temperature*
Salt and black pepper to taste

"ACTUALLY, I DON'T THINK I'D EVER SEEN A GROUSE BEFORE. I MEAN, NOT IN PERSON. A FEW TIMES IN A STILL LIFE AT THE MET. I'M PRETTY SURE THOSE WERE GROUSE. BUT THEY WERE USUALLY LYING ON A TABLE WITH SOME FRUIT."
—JOEL FLEISCHMAN

1 ♦ Preheat oven to 400°F.

2 ♦ Combine melted butter, cooked wild rice, celery, thyme, and marjoram in a bowl and mix well.

3 ♦ Loosely stuff mixture into the cavities of the grouse. Rub the skin of each bird with 1 tablespoon butter. Season to taste with salt and black pepper.

4 ♦ Place stuffed grouse in a shallow roasting pan so that birds are not touching. Roast for 10 minutes, lower heat to 350°F, and roast for 20 to 30 minutes more, until juices run clear when pierced with a fork.

MAKES 6 SERVINGS

CHICKEN-FRIED STEAK

From Maurice. He tells me he likes to serve it with potatoes au gratin. I haven't the heart to tell him the cream with the steak and the cheese with the potatoes are just too much together. At least they are for me.

I call for top round here, which is not exactly porterhouse, so this is as good a way to treat it as any. Add any spice mix you want for variety—Cajun, curry, whatever, just blend it with the flour. Goes splendidly with potatoes au gratin. Serve with a hearty red wine and a green salad. It isn't fancy but it's fast, fresh, and fills the void.

1 pound top round steak, cut into 4 pieces
5 tablespoons all-purpose flour
Salt and black pepper to taste
2 tablespoons vegetable shortening
1 cup heavy cream

1 ♦ Preheat oven to 200°F.

2 ♦ Place pieces of steak between sheets of waxed paper and pound thin with a mallet. Dredge with 3 tablespoons of the flour. Sprinkle liberally with salt and pepper.

3 ♦ Melt shortening in a cast-iron skillet over high heat. Add steak and cook for about 2 minutes per side, until golden brown. Transfer steak to a plate and place in oven to keep warm.

4 ♦ Add remaining 2 tablespoons flour to the skillet and cook for 2 minutes, stirring constantly. Continuing to stir, slowly add cream and cook until gravy has thickened.

5 ♦ Pour gravy over chicken-fried steak or serve on the side.

MAKES 4 SERVINGS

MOOSEBURGERS

Ed said he wanted to introduce this one. I found that quite touching.

I remember giving one of these to Dr. Fleischman when he first came to Cicely—after he waited all day for Elaine to get him out of his contract to be our doctor. She married some judge who died, and then she and Dr. Fleischman broke up, and he's still eating mooseburgers, so I guess everything turned out for the best. Oh, yeah, you can use ground chuck instead of moose. Except it's not the same.

*2 pounds ground lean moose fillet or lean
     ground chuck*
¼ cup pickle relish
2 tablespoons Dijon mustard
2 tablespoons catsup
½ teaspoon salt
⅛ teaspoon pepper
8 slices American cheese (optional)
8 hamburger buns
8 leaves lettuce
8 slices beefsteak tomato
8 thin slices red onion

1 ♦ Mix together ground moose fillet, relish, mustard, catsup, salt, and pepper.

2 ♦ Shape mixture into 8 patties and place on a hot grill (or in two hot skillets). Cook over medium-high heat for 4 minutes. Flip patties over, add a slice of cheese to each (if that's how you want it), and cook for 4 more minutes.

3 ♦ Place each burger on a bun and top with lettuce, tomato, and onion. Serve with fries and your choice of condiments.

MAKES 4–8 SERVINGS

RUTH-ANNE'S MEAT LOAF

1 large egg
1 teaspoon salt
¼ teaspoon ground black pepper
½ teaspoon dried thyme
2 tablespoons Dijon mustard
1 cup milk
½ cup chopped celery
½ cup chopped white onion
¼ cup plus 2 tablespoons catsup
1½ pounds ground chuck
1½ cups soft bread crumbs
3 strips uncooked bacon

1 ◆ Preheat oven to 350°F.

2 ◆ Beat egg lightly in a large bowl. Add salt, pepper, thyme, mustard, milk, celery, onion, and ¼ cup catsup, mixing ingredients well. Add chuck and bread crumbs and mix well until thoroughly combined.

3 ◆ Transfer mixture to a 9¼-inch loaf pan. Spread the remaining 2 tablespoons catsup over the loaf and top with bacon strips. Bake for 1 hour. Remove from oven and let set for 10 minutes before slicing.

MAKES 6–8 SERVINGS

THE BRICK'S SPAGHETTI AND MEATBALLS

I had to beg Holling to introduce this. He kept saying, "Ruth-Anne, for goodness' sake, it's just spaghetti and meatballs." Then he thought of something he wanted to add.

I'm no gourmet, but even I know the difference between Parmesan you grate yourself and that sawdust you shake out of the green foil can. Believe me, you really should go to the trouble of buying a wedge of the real thing. If you've never had it before you'll be amazed.

By the way, this is the dish that Joel and Maggie were having when they announced to everyone in the place that they'd had intimate relations. I remember that, because after their announcement I looked over at what they'd ordered and thought, "Could those meatballs use a little more Parmesan?"

1 cup Italian-flavored bread crumbs
1 pound ground beef
2 tablespoons grated Parmesan
1 large egg
1 clove garlic, peeled and chopped
½ teaspoon salt
⅛ teaspoon white pepper
3 tablespoons olive oil
1 cup finely diced yellow onion
1 cup finely chopped carrot
1 28-ounce can crushed tomatoes
2 8-ounce cans tomato sauce
1 teaspoon dried basil
3 drops hot sauce
1 8-ounce package dried spaghetti

1 ◆ In a large bowl, combine bread crumbs, ground beef, Parmesan, egg, garlic, salt, and pepper. Mix well.

2 ◆ Using your hands, shape beef mixture into 1-inch-thick meatballs.

3 ◆ Heat oil in a large frying pan over medium heat. Add meatballs and sauté, turning frequently, until meatballs are evenly browned (about 5 minutes). Using a slotted spoon, transfer meatballs to a plate and set aside.

4 ♦ Place onion and carrot in the frying pan and cook for 4 to 5 minutes, stirring constantly, until onion turns translucent. Stir in tomatoes with their liquid, tomato sauce, basil, and hot sauce. Add meatballs. Cover, reduce heat to low, and simmer for 1 hour, stirring occasionally.

5 ♦ After sauce has cooked for about 40 minutes, prepare spaghetti according to package directions. Drain well and place on a serving platter.

6 ♦ Pour meatballs and sauce over spaghetti and serve immediately.

MAKES 6 SERVINGS

ON BEING HUNGRY: AN EXCHANGE

Joel: You want steak. Thick, well-marbled, larded with fat, cholesterol, red dye number 5 . . .

Chris: Spaghetti. Starchy, al dente, maybe a nice pesto sauce.

Joel: Come on, Chris—not when you're really, really hungry. Not when you haven't eaten all day. You want flesh—flesh dripping in its own juices. Something with sinews. Something you've gotta tear with your teeth. The need for mastication is integral to the whole craving. Mandibles moving like pistons, triggering saliva . . .

Chris: I think the basic craving's more to have your stomach filled, preferably as fast as possible. Chewing just gets in the way. Plus, you can really pack your mouth full of spaghetti and just let it slide right down. Very efficient. None of that jaw syndrome thing. That's what you really want, Joel. The quick bulk-food thing.

RUTH-ANNE'S POT ROAST

The red meat scare has changed everybody's eating habits. There was a time when I butchered a whole heifer and two pigs a month. Now it's all turkey steaks and tofu sausage. Me, I'm from the real meat and real potatoes school. I want to eat what I want to eat. At my age I can live with a dormant sex life—but no pot roast is a sacrifice I'm not willing to make.

1 6-pound sirloin silver-tip roast
1 teaspoon coarse salt
½ teaspoon freshly ground black pepper
1 pound baby carrots, peeled and trimmed
1 tomato, sliced
12 small new red potatoes, scrubbed
12 small white onions, peeled
1 envelope packaged onion soup mix
1 cup red wine

1 ♦ Preheat oven to 375°F.

2 ♦ Line a large roasting pan with heavy-duty aluminum foil, leaving about 8 inches extra foil on each end. Place roast in center of the pan. Salt and pepper liberally and surround with the vegetables. Sprinkle soup mix evenly on top of everything in the pan and pour the wine over all.

3 ♦ Fold flaps of aluminum foil over to enclose roast and secure together. Close up sides. Bake for 1 hour, reduce heat to 250°F, and cook for an additional 2 hours.

MAKES 6–8 SERVINGS

SCHMULKE BERNSTEIN'S KOSHER SPARERIBS

Joel actually called his mother and asked her to get this recipe from Mr. Bernstein, who apparently is a real person.

OK, it's a gimmicky title but a dynamite recipe. Good luck finding lamb ribs in the store, but if you do, grab them. When I went with O'Connell to give a childbirthing class up north, she had everyone close their eyes and fantasize a good place. (No comment.) Eating these at Schmulke's is what I came up with. Try them and you'll see why.

4 pounds lamb ribs
1 white onion, peeled and quartered
1 teaspoon kosher salt
12 whole black peppercorns
1 bay leaf

BARBECUE SAUCE
½ cup honey
1 tablespoon cider vinegar
½ teaspoon dry mustard
¼ cup Worcestershire sauce
½ cup catsup
¼ cup chili sauce
2 cloves garlic, peeled and minced
2 tablespoons chopped white onion
⅛ teaspoon cayenne pepper

> "HERE'S A LITTLE-KNOWN BIBLICAL FACT. WHEN MOSES LED THE ISRAELITES OUT OF THE HOUSE OF BONDAGE, WHAT HE WAS REALLY LOOKING FOR WAS A PASTRAMI ON RYE FROM THE STAGE DELI."
> —JOEL FLEISCHMAN

1 ♦ Put ribs, onion, salt, peppercorns, and bay leaf into a large kettle. Cover with water and bring to a boil over high heat. Lower heat and simmer, uncovered, for 1 hour.

2 ♦ To make the sauce, combine all ingredients in a bowl and mix thoroughly. Transfer to a saucepan and simmer, uncovered, for 30 minutes over low heat.

3 ♦ Preheat broiler.

4 ♦ Line a broiling pan with aluminum foil. Transfer ribs to the broiling pan, discarding remaining ingredients in the kettle. Brush barbecue sauce on both sides of ribs, taking care to coat well. Broil for about 4 minutes on each side, until browned.

MAKES 6–8 SERVINGS

MAGGIE'S LEG OF LAMB

1 6-pound leg of lamb
3 cloves garlic, peeled and thinly sliced
1 lemon, cut in half
1 tablespoon dried rosemary
½ teaspoon ground black pepper

1 ◆ Preheat oven to 350°F. Line a roasting pan with aluminum foil and set aside.

2 ◆ With the point of a sharp paring knife, cut several diagonal slits, about ½ inch long, into lamb's surface. Stick a garlic slice into each slit. Squeeze lemon juice over lamb and rub rosemary and pepper over lamb's entire surface.

3 ◆ Place on a rack in the roasting pan and cook for 2 hours, to an internal temperature of 165°F. Serve with Maggie's Couscous (see Index).

MAKES 6–8 SERVINGS

SHELLY ON FOOD

Ask anybody and they'll tell you: I am NOT picky about what I eat. If something's made with like primo quality, hey, I'll do chomp time with the best of them. But as long as it's edible, I won't be insulted or offended or get all huffy, like Adam (although he's crazy) or Maurice. I figure, if it fills me up, and doesn't do a number on my buds going down, it's cool.

One thing I won't do, though, is eat competitively. Like when Wayne crammed in nine Kolossaburgers at the school fundraiser fair and tossed it all over the dash of his brother's new used car? That kind of scarf-and-barf routine is definitely not me.

RUTH-ANNE'S PORK CHOPS

A person my age grew up with the notion that pork was kind of a wicked food—tasty but fatty, low-down, and bad for you. Well, apparently it's a lot leaner now, which is nice.

This dish is as easy as pie, and it's delicious. It's still a favorite of my son Matthew, who's a bond trader in Chicago, and so has his pick of good restaurants . . . although his pick of careers still confounds me. I always wanted Matthew to be more like his brother, Rudy. Outdoorsy—a dreamer. But Matthew is a good son.

Now that I think of it, it's Rudy who likes the pork chops. Matthew likes the meat loaf.

Just don't try using ground ginger as a substitute for fresh. Pork is very forgiving, but some things are not negotiable.

3 tablespoons all-purpose flour
½ teaspoon salt
¼ teaspoon ground black pepper
6 1-inch-thick loin pork chops
2 tablespoons olive oil
1 tablespoon dark brown sugar
1 teaspoon grated fresh ginger
1 tablespoon grated orange zest
1 cup orange juice

1 ♦ Mix together flour, salt, and pepper. Dredge pork chops in flour mixture.

2 ♦ Heat oil in a large frying pan over medium heat. Brown chops in oil (about 8 minutes per side).

3 ♦ In a small bowl, combine remaining ingredients and mix well. Pour over pork chops. Bring to a boil, cover, reduce heat, and simmer until fork-tender (about 35 minutes). Serve with applesauce.

MAKES 6 SERVINGS

SHELLY'S HOT DOG AND CHEESE CASSEROLE

When Shelly gave me this recipe, she said she'd made it the night she demonstrated to Holling that she was mature.

I took it and said thank you.

This is what housewives served to their nuclear families in the fifties, before I was born. It's a little fancy for me, but when I made it for the Big H, I had something to prove.

1 8-ounce box elbow macaroni
½ pound hot dogs, sliced in rounds
2¼ cups shredded American cheese
5 tablespoons unsalted butter
1 small white onion, peeled and finely
    chopped
¼ cup all-purpose flour
2 cups milk
¼ teaspoon ground black pepper
½ teaspoon salt

1 ◆ Preheat oven to 350°F.

2 ◆ Cook macaroni according to package directions. Drain in a colander.

3 ◆ Put macaroni, hot dog rounds, and 2 cups of the cheese into a greased 2-quart casserole. Mix well.

4 ◆ Combine butter and onion in a medium-sized saucepan. Sauté over medium heat until onion is wilted (about 5 minutes). Whisk in flour. When flour is incorporated, remove from heat and slowly add milk while continuing to whisk. Return to heat, whisk in seasoning, and bring to a boil. Remove from heat and pour evenly over mixture in the casserole.

5 ◆ Sprinkle remaining cheese over the top and bake for 18 to 20 minutes, until cheese has melted and browned. Serve with catsup and a cold martini.

MAKES 4–6 SERVINGS

BLACK BEAN ENCHILADAS

Mrs. Noanuk contributed this gem and Ed volunteered to introduce it.

This is what Mrs. Noanuk cooked for Dr. Fleischman when he finished his fast before being inducted into our tribe. It's Mexican, except for the caribou. You can use ground chuck instead and, you know, it might even be better. Caribou is like all wild meat—almost too lean. Tasty, though.

Dr. Fleischman doesn't really do anything with the tribe. But I feel good knowing he's an honorary member.

1 pound lean ground caribou or lean
   ground chuck
2 teaspoons finely chopped garlic
2 tablespoons tequila
1 teaspoon chili powder
1 teaspoon ground cumin
1 teaspoon dried oregano
1 15-ounce can black beans, drained and
   rinsed
2 tablespoons vegetable oil
½ cup chopped white onion

1 8-ounce can tomato puree
1 16-ounce can whole peeled tomatoes
1 tablespoon red wine vinegar
1 teaspoon seeded and finely chopped
   jalapeño pepper
½ teaspoon salt
⅛ teaspoon black pepper
8 flour tortillas
½ cup chopped cilantro
1 cup grated Monterey Jack cheese

1 ♦ Preheat oven to 350°F.

2 ♦ Combine caribou, garlic, tequila, chili powder, cumin, and oregano in a heavy skillet. Sauté over low heat until meat is lightly browned (about 10 minutes). Mix in beans and set aside.

3 ♦ Heat vegetable oil in a frying pan over medium heat. Add onion and cook until golden (about 5 minutes). Add tomato puree and tomatoes, breaking tomatoes up with a wooden spoon. Add vinegar. Cook until liquid begins to boil. Stir in jalapeño, salt, and black pepper. Continue to cook until thickened (about 5 minutes).

4 ♦ Mound an equal amount of caribou mixture in the center of each tortilla. Roll each tortilla up and place in a 9″ × 13″ baking dish, seam side down. Pour tomato sauce over all. Sprinkle cilantro on top and cover with cheese.

5 ♦ Bake for 20 to 25 minutes, until cheese is bubbly and browned.

MAKES 4 SERVINGS

ADAM'S PUMPKIN TORTELLINI

Of course this is sublime—I remember Adam made it the first time he cooked at The Brick. I would have felt sorry for Holling, being upstaged so badly, if I hadn't been in heaven and unable to feel anything but delight. Still, it's work. So if you make it, go all the way and do the sauce, which is easy but unusual and helps amortize the labor on the tortellini.

Lightness, lightness, lightness. Yes, I know some people will think of this as being a sort of pumpkin pie pasta. Some people are MORONS.

TORTELLINI
1 cup semolina flour
1 cup all-purpose flour
3 large eggs, plus white of 1 large egg
1 cup pumpkin puree
2 tablespoons half-and-half
1 teaspoon ground nutmeg
1 tablespoon water

SAUCE
2 cups heavy cream
4 ounces goat cheese

1 ◆ Combine semolina flour and all-purpose flour in a food processor. Add the 3 whole eggs, one at a time, while pulsing.

2 ◆ Turn the small bits of dough out onto a floured board. Knead together into a single dough ball. Wrap and let sit for 30 minutes.

3 ◆ Cut dough ball into quarters. Flour and flatten each quarter into a pancake.

4 ◆ Dust the rollers of a manual pasta machine with flour. Adjust roller setting to the largest opening and work a flattened quarter of dough through the machine. Fold dough quarter in half and work through again. Repeat once more, then work through each successively smaller setting.

5 ◆ Repeat process for remaining 3 pieces of dough.

6 ◆ Cut 24 3-inch circles from each piece of dough after it has been worked through the smallest roller setting on the pasta machine.

7 ◆ For the filling, combine pumpkin, half-and-half, and nutmeg, mixing thoroughly.

8 ◆ Mound one-half teaspoonful of filling in the center of each circle of dough.

9 ♦ Whisk egg white with 1 tablespoon water. Using a pastry brush, paint the exposed surface around the mounds of filling with the egg-white mixture. Fold each circle in half to enclose filling, and pinch edges together to secure.

10 ♦ To form tortellini, shape each half circle around a finger, folding the pinched circular edges over to meet the straight border.

11 ♦ Put tortellini into a pan of boiling water. Cook over medium heat until they rise to the surface of the water, about 5 minutes.

12 ♦ To make the sauce, in a heavy saucepan, bring cream just to a boil over medium heat. Stir in goat cheese. Cook for about 2 minutes more, until mixture is thoroughly blended and heated. Pour over cooked tortellini.

MAKES 6 SERVINGS

MAURICE'S PASTA WITH CAYENNE TOMATO SAUCE

This is simplicity itself. (Frankly, I think it will go better with Maurice's Chicken-Fried Steak than those potatoes.)

Chris Stevens mentioned pasta all'arrabbiata to me once, and this is a variation on it. That uses red pepper flakes and parsley; this uses cayenne and basil. Find your own balance between the two. Any way you try it, this is proof that some vegetarian-type dishes can be satisfying to a palate that's not afraid of the full range of nourishment nature intended, i.e., that of the great American carnivore.

3 tablespoons extra-virgin olive oil
2 cloves garlic, peeled and finely chopped
4 pounds fresh plum tomatoes, peeled,
    seeded, and coarsely chopped
1 tablespoon chopped fresh basil
½ teaspoon cayenne pepper
½ teaspoon salt
1 pound fresh linguine

> **"HAVE YOU EVER TRIED EATING A REALLY BIG, SPICY MEAL RIGHT BEFORE BEDTIME? I FIND WHEN MY STOMACH'S UPSET, MY DREAMS ARE A LOT MORE INTENSE."**
> **— CHRIS STEVENS**

1 ◆ Heat oil in a large frying pan over medium heat. Add garlic and sauté until golden (about 5 minutes). Add tomatoes. Cook, stirring frequently, for about 10 minutes, until sauce begins to thicken. Stir in basil, cayenne pepper, and salt. Cook for an additional 3 minutes to allow flavors to blend.

2 ◆ While sauce is simmering, cook linguine according to package directions. Drain.

3 ◆ Put pasta into a large serving bowl. Pour sauce over pasta and toss. Serve with Maurice's Greens with Balsamic Vinaigrette (see Index).

MAKES 4-6 SERVINGS

6

SIDE DISHES

I DON'T LIKE THE IDEA OF "SIDE DISHES." WHY
NOT CO-EQUAL DISHES? BECAUSE MEAT IS
THE DADDY OF THE PLATE? SAYS WHO?
— MAGGIE O'CONNELL

CHRIS'S GLAZED CARROTS

The call for side dishes drew fewer than I would have hoped, but the range was good. Chris Stevens's contribution seems unlike him, although I'm not sure why I think that.

A couple years ago I lost my voice—completely, totally, summarily. To love, it turned out. I remember Maggie O'Connell was over to my place to fix the sink, and I served her dinner. (I wasn't in love with her—it's a long story.) This carrot dish was the supporting player to the lead of roast chicken.

A lot of people don't like cooked carrots. Neither do I, usually. But the honey here takes them all the way toward candied yams, and that flavor can be round and mellow and sweet enough to offer substantive support to a number of main dishes. Maggie thought so, too.

¼ *cup (½ stick) unsalted butter*
1½ *pounds baby carrots, peeled and*
     trimmed
3 *tablespoons honey*
¼ *teaspoon salt*
⅛ *teaspoon ground black pepper*

1 ♦ Melt butter in a large frying pan over medium heat. Add carrots. Cover, reduce heat, and simmer for 10 to 12 minutes, until fork-tender.

2 ♦ Add honey, salt, and pepper. Cook, stirring constantly, for another 1 to 2 minutes, until carrots are glazed.

MAKES 4–6 SERVINGS

RATATOUILLE

1 large eggplant, thinly sliced
1 teaspoon coarse salt
½ cup olive oil
2 white onions, peeled and thinly sliced
4 cloves garlic, peeled and chopped
2 zucchini, thinly sliced
1 red bell pepper, thinly sliced
1 green bell pepper, thinly sliced
4 tomatoes, peeled, seeded, and chopped
1 teaspoon salt
½ teaspoon freshly ground black pepper
1½ tablespoons chopped fresh basil
1 tablespoon chopped cilantro
½ pound white mushrooms, sliced

1 ◆ Put eggplant slices into a colander, add salt, and toss to coat. Set aside for 1 hour to drain.

2 ◆ After rinsing off salt, squeeze and drain excess water from eggplant.

3 ◆ Heat oil in a large, high-sided frying pan that has a cover. Add onions and sauté over medium heat for 3 minutes, until onions just begin to soften. Mix in eggplant, garlic, zucchini, and bell peppers. Cover and cook for 15 minutes.

4 ◆ Stir in tomatoes, lower heat, and simmer, uncovered, for 30 minutes.

5 ◆ Add all remaining ingredients, mix well, and cook, uncovered, for an additional 10 minutes.

MAKES 6–8 SERVINGS

WILD RICE STUFFING

Ed got this recipe from his Uncle Anku, who may have gotten it from his wife. In any case, it was used to stuff Joel's grouse—a phrase that sounds kind of vindictive, doesn't it?

I guess I should tell you that wild rice really isn't rice. It's a kind of grass. Still, I don't think that matters. This is a really good recipe, but remember everything that's in it. I mean, it's a meal in itself.

When we used it to stuff Dr. Fleischman's grouse, that was part of a big group meal at The Brick for Ruth-Anne's birthday party. So it was good that the stuffing was so rich. Plus wild grouse are kind of small. So this recipe is really good if you have some small birds you need to spread around a lot of people. Like grouse.

½ pound bulk Italian sausage
1 cup chopped white onion
½ cup chopped celery
2 pounds mushrooms (white button
     mushrooms or mixture of white and
     wild mushrooms), coarsely chopped
½ cup dry white wine
3 cups uncooked wild rice
4 cups homemade chicken stock or canned
     chicken broth
3 cups water
2 teaspoons chopped fresh thyme or
     ½ teaspoon dried thyme
1 teaspoon salt
½ teaspoon freshly ground black pepper
1 tablespoon unsalted butter

1 ♦ In a large skillet, sauté sausage over medium heat until cooked, but not browned. With a wooden spoon, transfer sausage to paper towels and drain.

2 ♦ Put 2 tablespoons of the fat left from cooking the sausage into a 3-quart saucepan. Add onion and celery and cook over medium heat until the onion begins to wilt (about 5 minutes). Stir in mushrooms and wine and cook until almost all of the liquid has been absorbed (about 10 minutes), stirring frequently.

3 ◆ Stir in wild rice and drained sausage. Continue to cook for 2 minutes, stirring constantly. Add chicken stock and water and bring to a boil. Cover, lower heat, and simmer for 45 minutes or until all liquid is absorbed. Remove the pan from heat and stir in thyme, salt, and pepper.

4 ◆ Preheat oven to 350°F.

5 ◆ Using half of the butter, grease a 12-cup (3-quart) casserole. Pour wild rice mixture into the dish. Cut up the rest of the butter and use to dot the top of rice mixture. Cover with aluminum foil and bake for 40 minutes.

MAKES 8–12 SERVINGS

MAGGIE'S COUSCOUS

2¼ cups homemade chicken stock or
canned chicken broth
2 tablespoons chopped fresh parsley
1½ tablespoons unsalted butter
1½ cups quick-cooking couscous

♦ Bring stock to boil in a medium-sized saucepan over high heat. Add all remaining ingredients, cover tightly, remove from heat, and let stand for 5 minutes. Serve immediately.

MAKES 6–8 SERVINGS

MAGGIE ON COOKING FOR ONE

Let's face it, it's hard. There's no sense of occasion when you eat alone—I mean, you're either going to be reading something or watching TV anyway, right? And even if you do go out of your way to make something good, you know you're stuck with the leftovers for days. And, of course, by the end of that period you're sick of it, since the thing that makes a special dish special is the thing you get tired of the fastest. Those unusual or distinctive flavors sort of nag at you, they demand attention that you just don't feel like giving anymore.

It's the boring things that you can eat over and over, isn't it? Is there a larger lesson in that for one's life? I hope not.

ADAM'S CUMIN NOODLES

Now this is wonderful. Don't tell Adam, but I went home and made this with just plain old linguine, and it was divine. It might even be better with Chinese water noodles, whatever they are. But it doesn't have to be.

This is the dish I taught that quack Fleischman when he shattered my solitude and dragged me back to this . . . this obscene riot of mass delusion that we're all agreeing to call contemporary civilization. . . . *Yes,* I taught him to cook this recipe in my shack, are you *deaf*? What do you mean, "I didn't have to"? You see all this, Miller? You note that I'm standing here within reaching distance of this cleaver? How sharp do you think I keep my cutlery?

½ pound fresh Chinese water noodles
2 tablespoons vegetable oil
½ pound boneless chicken breast, thinly
    sliced
1 tablespoon soy sauce
1 tablespoon sesame oil
2 teaspoons ground cumin
½ cup homemade chicken stock or canned
    chicken broth
2 green onions, cut into 1-inch pieces

1 ♦ Fill a 3-quart saucepan halfway with water and bring to a boil. Add noodles, bring back to a boil, reduce heat to medium, and cook for 5 minutes. Drain noodles in a colander and rinse under running water.

2 ♦ Heat oil in a wok or medium-sized frying pan over medium heat. Add chicken and cook for 2 minutes, stirring constantly. Add drained and rinsed noodles and all remaining ingredients. Raise heat to high and cook for another 2 minutes, stirring constantly. Serve immediately.

MAKES 4–6 SERVINGS

MARILYN'S SEASONED POTATOES

This is the potato dish that Marilyn serves all the time, to company as well as family. I know it's basic. Think of it as a foil for all the other fancy creations you plan to serve with it.

This is good.

12 small new potatoes
Salt

1 ◆ Wash and quarter potatoes. Place potatoes in a pot. Add water until potatoes are covered.

2 ◆ Boil potatoes for about 15 minutes, or until tender. Drain. Transfer potatoes to a serving dish. Salt and serve hot.

MAKES 4–6 SERVINGS

POTATOES AU GRATIN

Here are those potatoes of Maurice's that I've been talking about. It's a good solid version of something that really hits the spot, especially up here where it's cold. You might call it comfort food, which is a phrase I wouldn't be caught dead using, so pretend I didn't use it.

I remember I offered to cook this for Officer Barbara Semanski when she came investigating the theft of a radio from a truck of mine one Meltdown. That's when I first met that exceptional lady. I was feeling particularly uxorial and domestic that day—Meltdown'll do that to a man—but it occurs to me now that I may have made too housebroken an impression. On the other hand, had it not been Meltdown, I wouldn't have met her. So perhaps there really is a force that shapes our ends, rough-hew them though we may.

Sorry. Cookbook's no place to get sentimental.

2 tablespoons unsalted butter, at room
    temperature
6 large Idaho potatoes, peeled and cut into
    $\frac{1}{8}$-inch slices
1 cup shredded Swiss cheese
1 teaspoon salt
$\frac{1}{2}$ teaspoon ground black pepper
$\frac{1}{2}$ cup milk

1 ♦ Preheat oven to 375°F.

2 ♦ Coat the inside of a gratin dish liberally with the butter. Layer half the potato slices across the bottom of the dish and sprinkle half the cheese and half the salt and pepper on top. Layer the remaining potatoes and top with the rest of the cheese and salt and pepper. Pour the milk over all.

3 ♦ Cover with aluminum foil and bake for 50 minutes. Remove foil and continue baking until cheese has browned (about 5 minutes).

MAKES 6-8 SERVINGS

SHELLY ON FRENCH FRIES

I swear I think the main reason half the people eat at The Brick is for the fries. Not that they're all that primo or anything, although the frozen spirals can be excellent if Dave keeps the fryer at the right temperature and doesn't dump too many in at once. But the point is, who can make them yourself at home? It's kind of like a major injustice, that you have to go out for something so basic and important to human existence. So it gets to where you look forward to going out just so you can have fries!

Like this time Wayne got a fake ID and took me to this bar. He ordered boilermakers or some macho drink, and he wanted me to tank up, too. Well, I was hungry, but when I ordered, turned out, they didn't have a grill. Just sandwiches—and no fries! So I felt sad and pathetic instead of rollicking and loose. I had a Coke and we went home—and he blamed me!

LIGHTFEATHER DUNCAN'S MASHED POTATOES

Ed fell hard for Lightfeather, but it didn't work out, unfortunately. It seems she liked him more as a poet than as a boyfriend. I told him that one day he'd look back on that and laugh. He said he probably would, but that day hadn't come yet.

The girls and Father Duncan at the mission all like when I make this. It's no big deal. The horseradish was my idea. I did it as a joke and it went over really well. (Use white. The red kind looks strange.)

12 (about 3 pounds) medium-sized red potatoes
2 tablespoons olive oil
1 large yellow onion, peeled
¼ cup (½ stick) butter

1 cup sour cream
2 tablespoons prepared horseradish
1 tablespoon coarse-ground black pepper
2 teaspoons salt
1 cup shredded cheddar cheese

1 ◆ Preheat oven to 325°F.

2 ◆ Wash and quarter potatoes. Place in a large pot and cover with water. Boil potatoes until tender (about 15 minutes).

3 ◆ While potatoes are cooking, heat oil in a large skillet over medium-low heat. Coarsely chop onion and place in the skillet. Sauté until translucent (about 5 minutes).

4 ◆ Drain potatoes and place in a large mixing bowl. Add onion, butter, sour cream, horseradish, pepper, and salt. Using a hand-held electric mixer, whip potatoes until fairly smooth. Stir in cheese.

5 ◆ Transfer mixture to an ungreased casserole dish. Cover and bake for about 20 minutes, or until thoroughly heated.

MAKES 6–8 SERVINGS

7

BREADS

YOU KNOW, BREAD IS CONSIDERED THE SIMPLEST AND MOST BASIC OF FOODS, BUT ITS PROFOUND SECRET IS THAT IT'S JUST THE OPPOSITE. SEARCHERS FOR SIMPLICITY NEED LOOK NO FURTHER THAN FRUITS AND VEGETABLES, WHICH OF COURSE CAN BE EATEN AS IS. MEAT JUST NEEDS TO BE THROWN ON A FIRE. BUT BREAD NEEDS GRAIN, MILLING, YEAST, OVENS, AND EFFORT.

ANY ANIMAL CAN EAT PRODUCE OR FLESH. IT TAKES AN ENTIRE CIVILIZATION TO MAKE BREAD.

— CHRIS STEVENS

MAGGIE'S BRAN MUFFINS

I've always thought of muffins as something between bread and cake. The problem these days is that, in coffee shops and breakfast joints, even in good gourmet-ish places, the muffins they serve are the size of thatched huts. You cut one in half and it's more appealing to lie down on it and take a nap than to try to eat the whole thing. Fortunately, these don't seem quite so inflated.

1 cup all-purpose flour
2½ teaspoons baking powder
½ teaspoon baking soda
¼ teaspoon salt
¼ teaspoon ground cloves
¾ cup honey
¾ cup orange juice
1 cup oat bran
1 large egg, well beaten
¼ cup (½ stick) unsalted butter, melted
¼ cup dark molasses
1 cup dark raisins

1 ◆ Preheat oven to 375°F. Grease and flour a 12-cup muffin tin.

2 ◆ Sift flour, baking powder, baking soda, salt, and cloves together into a bowl. Set aside.

3 ◆ Whisk honey and orange juice together thoroughly. Mix in oat bran and continue to whisk until well blended.

4 ◆ In a large bowl, whisk melted butter into beaten egg. Thoroughly mix in molasses and then the oat bran mixture. Add flour mixture and stir with a wooden spoon until well blended. Fold in raisins.

5 ◆ Pour batter into the muffin tin, filling each cup ⅔ full. Bake for 25 to 30 minutes, until muffins begin to separate from the sides of the tin and a toothpick inserted into the center of a muffin comes out clean.

MAKES 12 MUFFINS

MAGGIE'S CORN MUFFINS

1⅓ cups white cornmeal
⅔ cup all-purpose flour
¾ teaspoon baking powder
1 teaspoon baking soda
1 teaspoon salt
2 large eggs, separated
1¾ cups buttermilk
¼ cup (½ stick) unsalted butter, melted

1 ◆ Preheat oven to 450°F. Lightly grease a 12-cup muffin tin.

2 ◆ Sift cornmeal, flour, baking powder, baking soda, and salt together into a large bowl.

3 ◆ In a separate bowl, beat egg yolks, and then thoroughly whisk in buttermilk and melted butter.

4 ◆ In a separate bowl, beat egg whites with an electric mixer until stiff (but not dry) peaks are formed.

5 ◆ Add buttermilk mixture to cornmeal mixture and blend until smooth and free of lumps. Using a slotted spoon, gently fold in egg whites.

6 ◆ Pour batter into the muffin tin, filling each cup ⅔ full. Bake for 12 to 15 minutes, until golden brown. Serve hot.

MAKES 12 MUFFINS

NEW YORK-STYLE BAGELS

Joel requested this recipe from his mother. I asked him if he had ever made these himself, but he just laughed.

You'd think, with the great abundance of salmon up here in Alaska, that some kind of natural selection process would have resulted in an accompanying availability of bagels. (For the benefit of the culturally deprived: salmon, when smoked, becomes lox. Lox is traditionally, if not exclusively, eaten on bagels.) But no; the culinary tradition in this neck of the woods as regards salmon is to dry it, flake it, and call the resulting leathery nuggets "Eskimo candy." Bagels, on the other hand, are one of the great foods of the western world—and, as such, are not on the menu here in Cicely.

Of course, the average New Yorker doesn't really make his or her own bagels. That's why God invented delicatessens.

1 potato, peeled and quartered
2 cups boiling water
1 package active dry yeast
4 cups all-purpose flour
½ tablespoon salt
1½ tablespoons sugar

¼ cup vegetable oil
2 large eggs
Cornmeal to dust cookie sheet
2 quarts water
1 egg white (optional)

1 ◆ Put potato into boiling water and boil for 15 minutes. Discard potato and let water cool to about 110°F.

2 ◆ Transfer ⅓ cup of the potato water to a small bowl. Sprinkle yeast over top of water and stir to combine. Set aside for 3 minutes.

3 ◆ Sift flour, salt, and ½ tablespoon of the sugar together into a large bowl. Add yeast mixture. Stir in another ⅔ cup of the potato water and the oil. Add eggs one at a time and stir briskly until a dough ball is formed.

4 ◆ Turn dough out onto a floured surface and knead for about 10 minutes until dough ball is firm, adding a little extra flour if needed. Place in a greased bowl, turning the dough so all sides are greased. Cover the bowl with a clean towel and set aside in a warm place for about 1 hour until dough has risen to double its original size. Punch the risen dough down to flatten and remove from the bowl.

5 ◆ Cut dough into 18 equal pieces and shape each piece into a 6- to 7-inch-long, ¾-inch-thick rope. Bring the ends of one rope together and pinch closed. (A little

water on the ends will help to secure them.) Repeat until 18 rings are formed. Cover all rings with the towel and let rise for 20 minutes.

6 ◆ Preheat oven to 450°F. Lightly grease a cookie sheet and dust with cornmeal.

7 ◆ Bring the 2 quarts water to a boil. Add the remaining tablespoon of sugar to the boiling water. Drop the bagels into the water one at a time, cooking each for 3 minutes, turning once. As each bagel is removed from the water, place it on the cookie sheet. If desired, paint the tops of the bagels with 1 egg white that has been beaten with 1 teaspoon water. Bake for 12 to 15 minutes, until golden brown.

MAKES 18 BAGELS

SAGE BREAD

This is a hearty, aromatic bread that's good for use in stuffings. But it's also good toasted with butter, and if you served a turkey sandwich on it nobody would ask any questions. Sage is a strong herb, especially when dried, so tread carefully.

This is what we used as the basis for the stuffing of Joel's grouse, by the way. But it's also good in fattier birds (it absorbs the juices). I know, I don't like the term "fattier birds" any more than you do, but that's what they are.

Cornmeal to dust cookie sheet
2½ cups warm (about 110° F) water
2 packages active dry yeast
7 tablespoons sugar
1 tablespoon salt
¼ cup vegetable oil
1 tablespoon dried whole sage leaves,
*   crumbled*
7 cups all-purpose flour
½ cup all-purpose flour, if needed
1 large egg (optional)

1 ◆ Lightly grease a cookie sheet and dust with cornmeal. Set aside.

2 ◆ Put ½ cup of the warm water into a small bowl. Sprinkle yeast over top of water and stir to combine. Set aside for 5 minutes.

3 ◆ In a large bowl, combine sugar, salt, and oil. Stir in sage and the remaining 2 cups warm water. Using a wooden spoon, stir in yeast mixture and 7 cups of flour. Let set for 10 minutes.

4 ◆ After 10 minutes, you should have a dough stiff enough to not stick to the fingers when formed into a ball. If needed, mix in the extra ½ cup flour.

5 ◆ Turn dough out onto a floured surface and knead for about 4 minutes until it is smooth, elastic, and satiny. Place dough ball in a greased bowl, turning the dough so all sides are greased. Cover the bowl with a clean towel and set aside in a warm place for about 1 hour, until the dough has risen to double its original size. Punch the risen dough down to flatten, and remove from the bowl.

6 ◆ Cut dough into 3 pieces lengthwise and shape each piece into a 10-inch strip. Lay the 3 strips side by side, about ½ inch apart, on the cookie sheet. Crimp strips

together at the top and braid. Tuck ends under. If desired, paint exposed surface of dough with an egg that has been beaten with 1 tablespoon water, using a pastry brush. Cover bread with the towel and let rise for 30 minutes.

7 ◆ Preheat oven to 350°F. Bake bread for 40 minutes, until it sounds hollow when lightly tapped on the bottom.

MAKES 1 LOAF

HOLLING ON WHY HE DOESN'T BAKE

I must say that, as much as I appreciate a home-baked bread, I have about as much desire to bake it myself for The Brick as I do to slaughter the hogs that provide us with our bacon. You may laugh, but I just don't like getting flour all over myself. I start to feel, well . . . feminine. And it's not the wearing of the apron that does it—I wear aprons all the time—it's that powdery sensation. If that means I'm a Neanderthal or somehow behind the times, so be it.

RYE CURRANT ROLLS

Maggie, again. Apparently this one brings back memories, so I'll shut up and let her tell you.

I spent my junior year abroad in Paris. At the time I wanted to be a baker. No desserts, no multilayered confections of cream and butter and sugar. Just bread and rolls. Back then I felt—at least I think I must have felt—that I could get away from my problems (family; men; family; the future; family) by immersing myself in something universal and fundamental. Some people try to get past their problems by being *above* them, with art or religion or meditation or whatever. I chose bread. I tried to get past my difficulties by going *under* them.

It didn't work, by the way. But I learned some great baking.

Cornmeal to dust cookie sheet
1½ cups warm (about 110°F) water
2 packages active dry yeast
¼ cup dark molasses
6 tablespoons sugar
2½ teaspoons salt
1 cup dried currants
1 tablespoon honey
3 cups rye flour
2 cups all-purpose flour
½ cup all-purpose flour, if needed

1 ◆ Lightly grease a cookie sheet and dust with cornmeal.

2 ◆ Put water into a large bowl. Sprinkle yeast over top of water and stir to combine. Set aside for 5 minutes.

3 ◆ Add molasses, sugar, salt, currants, and honey to yeast mixture. Mix together with a wooden spoon.

4 ◆ Sift rye flour into the mixture and blend until smooth. Sift 2 cups of the all-purpose flour into mixture and stir to combine thoroughly. This should produce a dough stiff enough to not stick to the fingers when formed into a ball. If needed, mix in the extra ½ cup flour.

5 ◆ Turn dough out onto a floured surface and knead for about 10 minutes until smooth and elastic. Place dough ball in a greased bowl, turning dough so all sides

are greased. Cover the bowl with a clean towel and set aside in a warm place for about 1 hour, until the dough has risen to double its original size. Punch the risen dough down to flatten and remove from the bowl.

6 ◆ Preheat oven to 375°F. Cut dough into 36 equal pieces, shape each piece into an oval, and place on the cookie sheet. Bake for about 20 minutes, until rolls sound hollow when lightly tapped on the bottom.

MAKES 36 ROLLS

BANANA BREAD A LA MAGGIE

Maggie is one of our best bakers, and this is one of her best recipes. The worst thing you can say about this recipe is, it shows how easy it is to make good banana bread. So if you're looking to promote your baking mystique, keep this hidden.

I like baking because it's a cross between cooking and wrestling. Not this recipe—no yeast, no punching down, it's fairly tame. But it's a good way to use up bananas that are getting black and too ripe.

I made this for Mike several times—you remember, Mike Monroe? What a great guy—and he loved it. Not that that's all that I did. Cook for him, I mean. In fact he cooked for me, too. So we were OK on that.

Mike's gone now, though. Not *gone* gone. I mean, he's still *alive*. He's in perfect health, in fact. He's just . . . gone.

2 cups all-purpose flour
2 teaspoons baking powder
½ teaspoon salt
⅔ cup sugar
2 large eggs
¼ cup (½ stick) unsalted butter, melted
⅓ cup buttermilk
1½ teaspoons ground cinnamon
¼ teaspoon ground nutmeg
1 cup mashed very ripe banana (2–3
    bananas)

1 ♦ Preheat oven to 375°F. Grease and flour a 9¼-inch loaf pan.

2 ♦ Sift flour, baking powder, salt, and sugar together into a bowl.

3 ♦ In a separate large bowl, beat eggs well with an electric mixer. Continue to beat while adding butter and then buttermilk. Add cinnamon, nutmeg, and banana, mixing well.

4 ♦ Add flour mixture and stir just until blended.

5 ♦ Pour batter into a prepared loaf pan. Bake for 50 to 60 minutes, until bread begins to separate from the sides of the pan and a toothpick inserted into the center comes out clean.

MAKES 1 LOAF

 8

DESSERTS

I DUNNO—THERE'S SOMETHING
INFANTILIZING ABOUT THE WHOLE IDEA OF
DESSERT. IT SEEMS TO COME AS A REWARD, A
PAYOFF FOR EATING YOUR MEAL. ADULTS
DON'T NEED THAT. SO MAYBE DESSERT
SHOULD BE SERVED FIRST. GRANTED, IT
WOULD RUIN YOUR APPETITE. BUT AT LEAST
YOU'D HAVE YOUR SELF-RESPECT.
> — JOEL FLEISCHMAN

BANANA CREAM PIE

¼ cup cornstarch
½ cup plus 2 tablespoons granulated
*   sugar*
½ teaspoon salt
2¼ cups milk
Yolks of 3 large eggs, beaten
¾ teaspoon vanilla extract
1 prepared 9-inch pie shell, baked and
*   cooled*
3 very ripe bananas, sliced into rounds
½ cup heavy cream
2½ tablespoons confectioners' sugar

1 ◆ Mix together cornstarch, granulated sugar, and salt in a small saucepan over medium heat. Gradually add the milk, stirring constantly, until the mixture is smooth, thick, and clear. Remove from heat.

2 ◆ In a medium-sized bowl, lightly beat egg yolks with a wire whisk. While continuing to whisk, add about one-third of the cornstarch mixture to yolks to blend. Stir mixture back into the saucepan.

3 ◆ Return the saucepan to medium heat, bring to a boil, and boil for 1 minute. Remove from heat and stir in vanilla extract. Pour half of the mixture into pie shell. Arrange banana slices on top and cover with remaining mixture. Refrigerate for at least 1 hour until well chilled.

4 ◆ Whip cream with confectioners' sugar. Spread evenly over chilled pie.

5 ◆ Refrigerate until ready to serve.

MAKES 1 PIE, ABOUT 6–8 SERVINGS

LEMON MERINGUE PIE

⅓ cup cornstarch
¼ teaspoon salt
2 cups granulated sugar
1½ cups boiling water
4 large eggs, separated
⅓ cup fresh lemon juice
1 teaspoon grated lemon zest
1 prepared 9-inch pie shell, baked and
    cooled

1 ♦ Preheat oven to 375°F.

2 ♦ Combine cornstarch, salt, and 1½ cups of the sugar in a small saucepan over medium heat. Gradually add boiling water, stirring until mixture is smooth, thick, and clear. Remove from heat.

3 ♦ In a small bowl, lightly beat egg yolks with a wire whisk. While continuing to whisk, add about one-third of the cornstarch mixture to yolks to blend. Stir mixture back into the saucepan.

4 ♦ Return the saucepan to medium heat and bring to a boil. Boil for 1 minute. Remove from heat and stir in lemon juice and zest. Pour into pie shell.

5 ♦ In a medium-sized bowl, beat egg whites until barely stiff. Add the remaining ½ cup sugar and continue to beat until stiff peaks are formed. Spread egg whites over pie, taking care to cover entire surface of pie and exposed crust.

6 ♦ Place in center of oven and bake for 9 to 10 minutes, until egg whites are golden brown. Remove from oven and cool on a wire rack.

MAKES 1 PIE, ABOUT 6–8 SERVINGS

HOLLING ON CREAM PIES

I suppose they're rather silly. You think of pie, you think of some dense, gooey suspension of apples or blueberries or cherries—mainly fruit. These are sort of mainly nothing—air, really, with some light whipped stuff around it. But I've developed a taste for these things, and the customers seem to like them too.

A person might ask, well, did your taste for this kind of dessert coincide with your relationship with Shelly? And the answer is, well, yes.

What you have to remember is, ever since my involvement with Shelly, I have been a happy man. And a happy man is a cream pie man.

MAURICE ON CREAM PIES

They're damned silly. A pie should have some heft, some meat, give you something to sink your teeth into. And you should be able to heat it up, maybe flip a dollop of ice cream on if you're feeling expansive. But you go to The Brick lately, all you see are these chiffon-meringue creations. That's not pie. That's a mirage of pie.

If I were some other man, I would attribute the downward slide of The Brick's dessert menu to the relationship between Holling and Shelly. But I have too much history, too big a vested interest, in that story to even pretend to be objective. So I'll keep my mouth shut and make my own pies at home.

SHELLY ON CREAM PIES

They're beyond silly, which is why I like them. Besides, you want a treat, you want that bliss-blast of sugar, right? But you *don't* want it sitting in your gut like a lump of cement, waiting to flab out your thighs. These pies make me at least think I'm getting away with something.

Dieting is psychological, anyway. Lots of people believe that you won't gain weight from food that no one sees you eat. Well, these pies are so light, it's easy to believe they won't make me a tubbo either. So far so good—at least, *I* think so. Usually.

HOLLING'S SPECIAL LIME CHIFFON PIE

½ cup water
1 envelope unflavored gelatin
⅛ teaspoon salt
½ cup fresh lime juice
4 large eggs, separated
1 cup sugar
1 tablespoon grated lime zest
2 drops green food coloring
¾ cup drained crushed unsweetened
    pineapple
1 prepared 9-inch graham cracker pie
    crust
1 cup heavy cream

1 ♦ Combine water and gelatin in a small bowl. Set aside.

2 ♦ In the top of a double boiler, over boiling water, combine salt, lime juice, egg yolks, and ½ cup of the sugar. Whisk just to combine. Add gelatin mixture and continue to cook, whisking constantly, until gelatin dissolves and mixture thickens slightly (about 5 minutes). Remove from heat and stir in lime zest and food coloring. Transfer to a large bowl and chill for 30 minutes. Spread pineapple evenly over bottom of pie shell. Set aside.

3 ♦ While egg yolk mixture chills, wash and dry the double boiler. In the top, over boiling water, beat egg whites to soft peaks with an electric mixer. Gradually add the remaining ½ cup sugar, beating until stiff (but not dry) peaks are formed. Remove from heat and gently fold into chilled egg yolk mixture. Pour into pie shell and refrigerate for at least 2 hours.

4 ♦ Just before serving, whip heavy cream and spread over top of pie.

MAKES 1 PIE, ABOUT 8 SERVINGS

ZABAGLIONE

To be honest, I don't know the latest wisdom on eating the egg yolks in this dreamy concoction from (who else?) Adam. But they do get cooked—don't they?—and in two kinds of wine. If alcohol has a sterilizing effect—oh, never mind.

Eve, my wife, likes this. When I met her she was a publicist for Knopf. I catered a publishing party for one of their authors *du jour*. You know, the latest twenty-four-year-old Ann Beattie clone? It's her first collection of paint-by-numbers, the *New-Yorker*-will-love-*this* stories? Where the characters are all just first names, and everyone is surrounded by brand names and is vaguely dissatisfied, and they watch Letterman and play "I've Got a Secret" but they can't *connect*? You're breaking my heart.

We went back to my place. I made this dish. We *connected*, okay?

And people wonder why nobody reads anymore.

Yolks of 8 large eggs
½ cup sugar
⅓ cup Marsala wine
1 tablespoon dry white wine
6 amaretti (amaretto-flavored Italian
*   cookies)*

1 ◆ Combine egg yolks, sugar, and wines in the top of a double boiler. Cook for about 10 minutes over boiling water, whisking constantly with a balloon whisk, until warm and thick (a spoonful will hold its shape). Remove from heat and continue to whisk until fluffy.

2 ◆ Spoon into six dessert glasses. Break up cookies and use to garnish the zabaglione. Serve immediately.

MAKES 6 SERVINGS

RUTH-ANNE'S CHEWY OATMEAL COOKIES

2 cups old-fashioned rolled oats
1½ cups all-purpose flour
½ teaspoon baking soda
1 teaspoon baking powder
½ teaspoon salt
1½ teaspoons ground cinnamon
1 cup (2 sticks) unsalted butter, at room
*   temperature*
½ cup dark brown sugar, firmly packed
½ cup granulated sugar
1 large egg
¼ cup milk
1½ teaspoons vanilla extract
1 cup pecan pieces
1 cup dark raisins

1 ♦ Preheat oven to 350°F.

2 ♦ Mix together oats, flour, baking soda, baking powder, salt, and cinnamon. Set aside.

3 ♦ In a large bowl, cream butter while slowly adding both sugars. Continue to beat until mixture is light and fluffy. Blend in egg, milk, and vanilla extract. Add oat mixture, pecans, and raisins, stirring to blend.

4 ♦ Drop batter by the tablespoonful, about 2 inches apart, onto an ungreased cookie sheet. Bake for 12 to 15 minutes, until golden brown. Remove cookies from the sheet and allow to cool on a rack.

MAKES ABOUT 48 COOKIES

MAGGIE'S FUDGE

It's nice to have a candy recipe in here. It's disturbing to think that, somewhere, someone is actually cooking things like Milky Ways or Baby Ruths. Actually it's hard to believe. But this is so simple even I can make it.

I know: fudge. It's so dense and sweet, it's not exactly something you can dig into. I made it for Bruce—OK, the late Bruce—and he called it "the plutonium of candy." Not because it was toxic, mind you, but because a little goes a long way. How much of it can you eat before a two-pound slab of it dries up?

So give it away. It's perfect for cutting into bricks and wrapping (first plastic wrap, then something decorative) and handing out. Each person gets enough for a good sampling but not so much that they start to feel guilty either from having eaten all of it or NOT having eaten all of it. You feel generous. And no one but the cook knows how easy it was to make.

½ cup plus 1 tablespoon unsweetened
    cocoa powder
3 cups sugar
¼ teaspoon salt
1 cup milk
1 tablespoon light corn syrup
¼ cup (½ stick) unsalted butter
1 teaspoon vanilla extract
1 cup chopped walnuts

1 ◆ Lightly grease an 8-inch square baking pan.

2 ◆ Combine cocoa, sugar, salt, milk, corn syrup, and butter in a 3-quart saucepan. Cook over medium heat, stirring occasionally with a wooden spoon, until sugar has dissolved.

3 ◆ Continue to cook, stirring occasionally, until a "soft ball" stage is reached. To test for the soft ball stage, have a glass of water handy. When fudge looks thick, remove from heat and spoon a little into the water. A ball should form that will feel soft when picked up. If the soft ball doesn't form, return fudge to heat and continue to cook.

4 ◆ Once the soft ball stage is reached, remove fudge from heat and allow to cool. Do not stir.

5 ◆ When bottom of the pan feels lukewarm, stir in vanilla extract and nuts. With a wooden spoon, beat until mixture loses its gloss and becomes creamy.

6 ◆ Pour into prepared pan and smooth out evenly. Refrigerate at least 3 hours. Cut into squares.

MAKES ABOUT 2 POUNDS

RUTH-ANNE'S BIRTHDAY CARROT CAKE

About that name: I insisted that it just be called Carrot Cake. But Shelly, who painstakingly followed this recipe which her cousin had faxed her, insisted, too—that it include my name on it or she'd withdraw the recipe. So what could I do? It was served at my birthday party on the day Ed presented me with a plot of land for my grave. So it has pleasant associations for me.

My cousin Ginny got this from her stepmother. It's got two cups of grated carrot in it, but that's OK. For fun it's got all those fruits and nuts. Plus, what wipes me is, NO SUGAR. Except for the icing.

I had a blast making this for Ruth-Anne. It's easy to say that old people are a drag, since they're usually your parents, and it's a kid's job to realize that her parents are a drag. But Ruth-Anne is so old she's, like, beyond parenthood, to where she's just this cool elderly American.

CAKE
2¼ cups all-purpose flour
1 teaspoon baking powder
1½ teaspoons baking soda
½ teaspoon salt
1 teaspoon ground cinnamon
½ teaspoon ground nutmeg
½ teaspoon ground cloves
1 cup plus 2 tablespoons vegetable oil
3 large eggs, lightly beaten
1 teaspoon vanilla extract
2 cups finely grated carrot
1 8-ounce can crushed pineapple, well
    drained
2 tablespoons lemon juice
1 cup coarsely chopped pecan pieces
1 cup golden raisins
1 cup flaked coconut

FROSTING
1 8-ounce package cream cheese
¼ cup milk
1½ teaspoons vanilla extract
¼ teaspoon allspice
2 cups confectioners' sugar

GARNISH
75 birthday candles

1 ♦ Preheat oven to 350°F. Grease and flour two 9-inch round layer cake pans.

2 ♦ Combine flour, baking powder, baking soda, salt, and spices in a large bowl and mix together thoroughly. Beat in oil until well incorporated. Add eggs and beat well. Add all remaining ingredients and stir until well mixed. Divide batter evenly between the two pans.

3 ♦ Bake for 45 to 55 minutes, until a toothpick inserted into the center of each layer comes out clean.

4 ♦ Remove both pans from the oven, transfer to a rack, and cool for 20 to 30 minutes. Turn cakes out of the pans onto the rack and allow to cool completely.

5 ♦ To make the frosting, beat cream cheese and milk with an electric mixer until smooth. Beat in vanilla extract and allspice. Gradually add confectioners' sugar, while continuing to beat.

6 ♦ Place one cooled layer on a serving plate and spread frosting on top of it. Set other cooled layer on top of frosted first layer and frost the top and outside of the whole cake. Garnish with birthday candles and serve.

MAKES 1 CAKE, ABOUT 8–12 SERVINGS

9

THANKSGIVING

WHY DO WE EAT? BECAUSE SENSITIVE PEOPLE DISCOVER THEY HARBOR A SINCERE FEELING OF GRATITUDE BUT NO CREDIBLE DEITY TO EXPRESS IT TO. FOR THIS GREAT BIG "THANK YOU" WE CRAVE A "YOU'RE WELCOME," BUT WHO OR WHAT IS IT GOING TO COME FROM? FATE IS OUT, "THE GODS" ARE ACTORS IN A RAY HARRYHAUSEN MOVIE. WE'RE LIKE STORM CLOUDS CHARGED WITH STATIC, DESPERATE TO UNLEASH IT. WHAT ELSE IS THERE BUT TO STUFF YOURSELF INTO A STUPOR?

— CHRIS STEVENS

TACO SALAD WITH FRESH GUACAMOLE

When we have our town Thanksgiving feast at The Brick, Shelly contributes this. And if you think that it isn't picked clean within minutes, by people desperate for something other than turkey, you're from out of town.

This is your standard taco salad. I suggest a layering thing for presentation: chips on the bottom, lettuce overlapping, with a border of chips and lettuce showing. I'm not normally that fussy, but hey, this is Thanksgiving.

1 14–16-ounce bag taco chips
2 heads red leaf lettuce, shredded (about 6 cups)
2 cups shredded cooked chicken breast
½ cup finely chopped white onion
3 cups chopped tomatoes
3 cloves garlic, peeled and finely chopped
½ teaspoon salt
1 cup chopped cilantro
3 fresh jalapeño peppers, seeded and finely chopped
¼ teaspoon sugar
¼ cup fresh lime juice
2 cups grated Monterey Jack cheese
2 cups Fresh Guacamole (recipe follows)
¾ cup sliced black olives

> "IT'S GETTING TO BE THAT DAY OF THE YEAR, FOLKS, WHEN THE GRIM REAPER MEETS MILES STANDISH, AND DEATH'S HEAD PUMPKINS ABOUND. YES, CICELY, WE'RE FAST APPROACHING THE FOURTH THURSDAY OF NOVEMBER THAT MS. SARAH J. HALE PROMOTED INTO THE HALLOWED HALLS OF HOLIDAYHOOD— THANKSGIVING. A WORD OF CAUTION TO ALL OF US WHITE FOLK OUT THERE: THE TOMATOES ARE STARTING TO FLY, SO KEEP ON DUCKING."
> —CHRIS-IN-THE-MORNING

1 ◆ Line a large platter with taco chips. Spread lettuce over chips, leaving a 1-inch border of chips. Set aside.

2 ◆ Toss together all remaining ingredients except cheese, guacamole, and olives. Spread mixture over lettuce, leaving a 1-inch border of lettuce. Sprinkle cheese on top. Spread guacamole evenly over cheese. Garnish with sliced olives.

MAKES 8–12 SERVINGS

FRESH GUACAMOLE

2 large very ripe avocados
2 tablespoons fresh lime juice
1 cup diced tomatoes
½ cup diced white onion
2 teaspoons seeded and finely diced
*   jalapeño pepper*
4 drops hot sauce
2 tablespoons chopped cilantro

♦ Place peeled and pitted avocados into a bowl. Mash with a large fork, add lime juice, and mix well. Add all other ingredients and mix thoroughly.

MAKES ABOUT 2 CUPS

ROAST TURKEY WITH GIBLET GRAVY

1 12-pound fresh turkey
1½ teaspoons coarse salt
1 teaspoon freshly ground black pepper
½ cup (1 stick) unsalted butter, at room
*   temperature*
4 cloves garlic, peeled and crushed
1 yellow onion, peeled and chopped
1 carrot, peeled, trimmed, and chopped
1 rib celery, chopped
3 tablespoons chopped fresh sage or 3
*   teaspoons dried sage*
1¼ cups dry white wine

1 ◆ Preheat oven to 350°F.

2 ◆ Remove giblets (gizzard, liver, heart) and neck from turkey. Refrigerate until ready to prepare Giblet Gravy (recipe follows). Rinse turkey under cold running water, inside and out. Pat dry with paper towels, making sure skin is dry.

3 ◆ Liberally rub salt and pepper inside the cavity and on the outside of turkey. With fingertips, rub butter into the skin of the bird, using at least half on the breast portion. Fold wings under bird. Place on a rack in a roasting pan.

4 ◆ In a bowl, mix together garlic, onion, carrot, celery, sage, and ¼ cup of the wine. Pour mixture into the cavity of the turkey. Place a small piece of aluminum foil over cavity opening. Tie legs together with a piece of clean string.

5 ◆ Pour the remaining cup of wine into the bottom of the pan. Take a piece of aluminum foil large enough to cover the total girth of the turkey and fold in half to create a tent when it is reopened. Lay the tent across the center section of the bird, over the breast, making sure that it is open at both ends.

6 ◆ Place turkey in oven and roast for about 3½ hours (18 minutes per pound) or until an instant-read thermometer inserted at the fleshiest part of the thigh, away from bone, reads 175°F and the juices run clear. As turkey roasts, baste every 20 to 30 minutes with pan juices. When the turkey is about three-quarters cooked, remove the aluminum foil tent to allow the breast skin to brown.

7 ◆ Remove cooked turkey from oven, transfer to a cutting board, and loosely cover with the aluminum foil tent. Let turkey set for 20 minutes before carving.

8 ◆ Reserve pan juices for making gravy (see next recipe).

MAKES 8-14 SERVINGS

GIBLET GRAVY

Giblets and neck from a 12-pound turkey,
   trimmed
2 cups homemade chicken stock or canned
   chicken broth
1 cup dry white wine
Pan juices from roasted turkey (see
   previous recipe)

1 ◆ After turkey has cooked for 2 hours (see previous recipe), place trimmed giblets and neck in a small saucepan with stock and wine. Bring to a boil over medium heat. Lower heat and simmer for 1½ hours.

2 ◆ When turkey is done and has been removed from the roasting pan, strain pan juices into a measuring cup and transfer to a food processor or blender. Add enough simmering liquid from the giblet pot to make 4 cups total liquid. Coarsely cut up giblets and neck meat and add to liquid. Process until smooth and thick. Pour into the roasting pan and cook for 5 minutes over medium heat, scraping occasionally with a spatula to dislodge any particles that have adhered to the bottom of the pan. When gravy is thick and hot, pour into a server.

MAKES ABOUT 4½ CUPS

MIKE'S EGGPLANT PARMESAN

Mike Monroe is usually a vegetarian. (Can you say that? Or is it like saying of a girl that sometimes she's a virgin?) This is a basic recipe he left before taking off to clean up the world. You can jazz it up at will. I'll let you even if he wouldn't.

Last Thanksgiving in Cicely was something of a benchmark for me. I had so much to be thankful for. I left my house. I had a glass of water at The Brick with Maggie—complete with a piece of lemon I'm *pretty sure* hadn't been washed. Sure, I had a turkey drumstick and paid for it, retail, the next day. But I ate bread AND BUTTER and got away with it. Pretty much.

2 large eggs, beaten
¼ cup milk
¼ cup olive oil
1 large eggplant, cut into ½-inch slices
1½ cups Italian-flavored bread crumbs
1 teaspoon dried oregano
½ teaspoon garlic powder
2 cups tomato sauce
1 cup grated mozzarella cheese
¼ cup grated Parmesan

1 ♦ Preheat oven to 350°F. Lightly grease a 13″ × 10″ × 2″ baking dish.

2 ♦ Whisk beaten eggs and milk together in a bowl.

3 ♦ Heat oil in a frying pan over medium heat.

4 ♦ Dip eggplant slices into egg and milk mixture, roll in bread crumbs to coat, and cook in heated oil for about 2 minutes per side, until golden brown. Remove from heat and drain on paper towels.

5 ♦ Layer eggplant into the prepared baking dish. Sprinkle seasonings onto the slices, pour tomato sauce over all, and top with mozzarella and Parmesan.

6 ♦ Cook, uncovered, for about 20 minutes, until cheese has melted and browned and eggplant is fork-tender.

MAKES 4–6 SERVINGS

CANDIED YAMS

10–12 (about 6 pounds) medium-sized
   yams
1 cup water
2 cups dark brown sugar, firmly packed
½ teaspoon salt
¼ cup (½ stick) unsalted butter
½ cup chopped pecans

1 ◆ Peel yams and halve lengthwise.

2 ◆ In a large saucepan, bring water, sugar, and salt to a boil over medium heat. Add yams and stir to coat all sides. Cover, reduce heat to low, and simmer for about 1 hour, turning yams a few times, until just fork-tender. Add butter and pecan pieces, mix well, and continue to cook for 5 minutes.

3 ◆ Transfer yams to a serving dish. Spoon a little syrup and some pecan pieces over each yam half and serve.

MAKES 10–12 SERVINGS

MAGGIE ON THANKSGIVING

As Fleischman will tell you, my family would not be at the top of your list of groups with which to spend Thanksgiving *once*, let alone eighteen consecutive years of precollege youth.

Here we were, in the upper one-zillionth percentile of the American socioeconomic scale, as secure as it was possible to be in '60s America, and my parents' observance of Thanksgiving was as rigid as the Changing of the Guard. Turkey. Sweet potatoes. Cranberry sauce. Green beans. The same wine every year. Pumpkin chiffon pie and spice cookies. Constant Comment tea.

The conversation was ostensibly an appreciation of "all we have to be thankful for," but, the way my father led in the recitation of our blessings, it was more like an inventory of assets to be defended at gunpoint. My mother smiled with forced cheer, my brother smirked a lot. I sighed and felt put-upon.

What's the difference between observing tradition and placating the gods? It's your attitude, isn't it? My attitude today is, thank God (or, the Gods) for plantains on Thanksgiving!

PLANTAINS

4 *plantains, fully ripe and blackened*
1 *cup all-purpose flour*
2 *cups vegetable oil*
2 *limes, quartered*

1 ♦ Peel plantains. Cut on the diagonal into thin slices. Place flour in a shallow bowl and dredge plantain slices on all sides.

2 ♦ In a heavy frying pan, heat oil over medium heat. (Oil is hot enough for cooking when a few drops of water sprinkled on top cause oil to crackle and bubble up slightly.) Put a few of the dredged plantain slices into the oil and fry just until golden (about 2 minutes). Remove from oil and drain on paper towels. Continue until all slices are fried. Serve warm with lime wedges.

MAKES 8–12 SERVINGS

BAKED LENTILS

Holling does these up every Thanksgiving. Each time I realize how easy it would be to make this myself at home. And each year, after Thanksgiving, I forget about it.

I don't come from what you would call a lentil background. But one winter, when I was trapping beaver, I took shelter from a blizzard in a cabin with a man from Poland. He showed me these. We were snowed in, and pretty much couldn't go anywhere for three days. You can get to know someone fairly well in the course of a three-day emergency, and when I walked out of that cabin once the storm passed, I knew I'd never forget that fellow.

But I did, actually. I've forgotten him completely. His face, his name—the specifics of the man are a complete blank in my mind. The only thing I remember is the lentils. I still can't decide whether that story is one of hope or futility.

3 cups dried lentils
3 cups water
6 cups homemade chicken stock or canned
  chicken broth
1 teaspoon salt
¼ teaspoon ground black pepper

12 slices crisply cooked bacon, crumbled
1 cup finely chopped white onion
¼ cup honey
1 cup bread crumbs
¼ cup (½ stick) unsalted butter, melted

1 ◆ Place lentils in a colander and wash under running water. Drain. Transfer lentils to a large bowl and add enough water to cover lentils by 1 inch. Allow to soak 8 hours or overnight.

2 ◆ Preheat oven to 350°F.

3 ◆ Drain lentils. Place in a 3-quart saucepan. Add chicken stock and salt and bring to a boil over medium heat. Cover, lower heat, and simmer for 15 minutes, until tender.

4 ◆ Remove from heat. Stir in pepper, bacon, onion, and honey. Transfer to a large greased casserole.

5 ◆ In a separate bowl, mix bread crumbs and butter together. Spread over the top of casserole. Bake for 20 to 25 minutes, until top is browned.

MAKES 8–12 SERVINGS

MAURICE'S THANKSGIVING BENEDICTION TO NATIVE AMERICANS

Thanksgiving in Cicely, as you may know, is when the Native American population takes it upon themselves to hurl tomatoes at us white folk. With impunity.

You want to know what I think, I think it's childish. I'd be the last to deny the history of oppression and pillage that Indians have suffered at the hands of my ancestors. But I mean, come on. This isn't vaudeville. You're not chasing some bad baggy-pants off the stage to get to the tootsie with the pasties. This is life!

Get an education, get a job, work your way up, take some risks. Stay off the sauce and grab for the gusto. What I'm saying is, don't get mad. Get even. Then you can tell the rest of the world to go to hell.

Not the most pious Thanksgiving sentiment in the world, but I stand by it.

SAFFRON RICE

¼ cup virgin olive oil
1 cup chopped white onion
3 cloves garlic, peeled and finely chopped
1 small red bell pepper, chopped
1 small yellow bell pepper, chopped
3 cups long-grain white rice
1 bay leaf
6½ cups homemade chicken stock or
*   canned chicken broth*
1 teaspoon saffron threads
½ cup chopped pimiento-stuffed green
*   olives*
¼ cup slivered blanched almonds

1 ◆ In a heavy 3-quart saucepan, heat oil over medium heat. Add onion, garlic, and bell peppers and sauté until vegetables have wilted (about 10 minutes). Add rice and bay leaf, stir, and continue to sauté for 5 minutes, until rice turns translucent.

2 ◆ Add stock and saffron and bring to a boil. Cover, lower heat, and simmer for 20 minutes, until all liquid has been absorbed and rice is tender. Remove from heat, discard bay leaf, and fluff rice with a fork.

3 ◆ Transfer to a serving bowl and garnish with olives and almonds.

MAKES 8–12 SERVINGS

MARILYN ON THANKSGIVING

The only group of creatures with less reason to celebrate Thanksgiving than Native Americans are turkeys.

RISOTTO

6 *cups homemade chicken stock or canned*
   chicken broth
¼ *cup virgin olive oil*
2 *cups chopped white onion*
2 *cups Arborio rice or other short-grain*
   rice
1 *cup dry white wine*
¼ *cup minced fresh chives*
½ *teaspoon salt*
¼ *teaspoon freshly ground black pepper*
¾ *cup freshly grated Parmesan*
¼ *cup chopped Italian parsley*

1 ◆ Bring chicken stock to a boil in a saucepan over medium heat. Lower heat and maintain a simmer.

2 ◆ Heat oil in a heavy, straight-sided saucepan over medium heat. Add onion and sauté over low heat for 5 minutes or until wilted. Add rice and cook, stirring often, for 5 minutes.

3 ◆ Slowly add 1½ cups of the hot stock to the rice, stirring constantly. Allow mixture to come to a simmer. Once stock has been absorbed, add another 1½ cups of stock, stirring constantly, and bring back to a simmer. When this additional stock has been absorbed, stir in wine and chives. Continue adding the remaining stock, ½ cup at a time, stirring constantly, until rice is creamy and tender. (This whole process, from addition of the first 1½ cups of stock, should take 20 to 25 minutes.) Stir in salt and pepper.

4 ◆ Transfer to a serving bowl and garnish with Parmesan and parsley. Serve immediately.

MAKES 8–12 SERVINGS

CRANBERRY-WALNUT RELISH

2 navel oranges
3 cups fresh cranberries
1 cup apricot preserves
½ cup chopped walnuts

1 ◆ Cut unpeeled oranges into quarters, and remove seeds with the tip of a sharp knife. Place in a food processor and coarsely chop. Add cranberries and preserves and process until finely chopped.

2 ◆ Transfer to a serving bowl and stir in walnuts. Refrigerate until ready to serve.

MAKES ABOUT 4½ CUPS

CHRIS ON PRIORITIES

I read once about a preindustrial tribe—maybe the notoriously nasty Ik, maybe not—for whom the chief problem and overriding obsession of daily life was the acquiring of enough to eat. Consequently—contra Freud—these people did not dream about sex. They dreamt about food.

There's a message in there somewhere for us. I think it's that the supposedly elevated center of being, the mind and consciousness, is only free to indulge in sensual fantasies and surrealist recreation once the belly is full. The mind cavorts only with the body's permission.

So dig in, Descartes. You think, therefore you are. But you eat, therefore you think.

DAY OF THE DEAD SUGAR COOKIES

4 cups all-purpose flour
1 teaspoon baking powder
¾ teaspoon baking soda
½ teaspoon salt
1 cup (2 sticks) unsalted butter, at room temperature
1½ cups sugar
2 large eggs
¼ cup milk
1 teaspoon vanilla extract
2 teaspoons grated lemon zest

1 ◆ In a large bowl, sift together flour, baking powder, baking soda, and salt. Set aside.

2 ◆ In a separate large bowl, beat butter, sugar, and eggs with an electric mixer until light and fluffy. Add milk, vanilla extract, and lemon zest and mix until smooth. Continue beating while gradually adding flour mixture. When flour is completely incorporated, gather dough into a ball, wrap in waxed paper, and refrigerate for at least 3 hours.

3 ◆ When ready to bake cookies, preheat oven to 375°F.

4 ◆ Remove dough ball from the refrigerator, cut into 4 equal pieces, and return 3 of the pieces to the refrigerator.

"THANKSGIVING. I LOVE IT. IT'S THE ONE HOLIDAY THAT'S FOR EVERYONE . . . CHRISTIAN, JEW, MUSLIM, MOONIE—NO ONE'S LEFT OUT IN THE COLD. ONE OF THE THINGS THAT ALWAYS INTRIGUED ME AS A KID WAS TRACING YOUR HAND AND MAKING A TURKEY OUT OF IT. IT HAD GREAT SIGNIFICANCE IN MY LIFE. I MEAN, HERE I WAS, THIS KID WITH LITTLE OR NO ARTISTIC TALENTS WHATSOEVER, NOT ABLE TO DRAW A STICK, LET ALONE A STICK <u>MAN</u>, AND SUDDENLY, HERE'S A THANKSGIVING TURKEY. AND I DID IT.
PILGRIMS, INDIANS, THE MAYFLOWER . . . THEY'RE ALL VIVID, HAPPY IMAGES THAT YOU NEVER LOSE. DOESN'T MATTER WHAT'S ON THE TABLE—IT'S THE CELEBRATION ITSELF THAT'S SO GREAT."
—JOEL FLEISCHMAN

5 ♦ On a well-floured surface, roll out the first piece of dough to a thickness of ¼ inch. Using 2½-inch cookie cutters, cut out decorative shapes. One at a time, remove the remaining pieces of dough from the refrigerator and repeat the process.

6 ♦ Place cookies on lightly greased cookie sheets, 2 inches apart. Bake for 10 to 12 minutes, until golden.

MAKES ABOUT 48 COOKIES

CHRIS'S PUMPKIN PIE

2 large eggs
¾ cup dark brown sugar, firmly packed
1½ teaspoons ground ginger
1½ teaspoons ground cinnamon
½ teaspoon salt
1 16-ounce can pure pumpkin
1½ cups evaporated milk
¼ cup orange juice
2 prepared 9-inch pie shells, baked and
    cooled
White of 1 large egg, beaten

"PEOPLE, THE MELLOW SWEETNESS OF PUMPKIN PIE OFF THE METAL TANGINESS OF A PRISON SPOON IS SOMETHING YOU WILL NEVER FORGET . . ."
—CHRIS STEVENS

1 ♦ Preheat oven to 450°F.

2 ♦ In a large bowl, beat eggs lightly. Add sugar, ginger, cinnamon, salt, pumpkin, milk, and orange juice. Mix with a wooden spoon until smooth.

3 ♦ Lightly brush pie shells with beaten egg white. Pour half the pumpkin mixture into each shell.

4 ♦ Place a heavy cookie sheet into the oven for 5 minutes to preheat. Place pies on the cookie sheet and bake for 10 minutes. Reduce heat to 300°F and bake for about 45 minutes more, until the tip of a sharp knife inserted into the center of each pie comes out clean.

MAKES 2 PIES, ABOUT 12–16 SERVINGS

🦌 10 🦌
CHRISTMAS IN CICELY

I LIKE CHRISTMAS, BUT I'M NOT A CHRISTIAN,
IN THE SAME WAY THAT I LIKE HALLOWEEN,
BUT I'M NOT DEAD.

— ED CHIGLIAK

"A LONG TIME AGO, THE RAVEN LOOKED DOWN FROM THE SKY AND SAW THAT THE PEOPLE OF THE WORLD WERE LIVING IN DARKNESS. THE BALL OF LIGHT WAS KEPT HIDDEN BY A SELFISH OLD CHIEF. SO THE RAVEN TURNED HIMSELF INTO A SPRUCE NEEDLE AND FLOATED ON THE RIVER WHERE THE CHIEF'S DAUGHTER CAME FOR WATER. SHE DRANK THE SPRUCE NEEDLE. SHE BECAME PREGNANT AND GAVE BIRTH TO A BOY—WHICH WAS THE RAVEN IN DISGUISE. THE BABY CRIED AND CRIED UNTIL THE CHIEF GAVE HIM THE BALL OF LIGHT TO PLAY WITH. AS SOON AS HE HAD THE LIGHT, THE RAVEN TURNED BACK INTO HIMSELF AND CARRIED THE LIGHT INTO THE SKY. FROM THEN ON, WE NO LONGER LIVED IN DARKNESS."

—MARILYN WHIRLWIND

RUTH-ANNE'S RAVEN BREAD

Around Christmastime our Native American population celebrates the legend of the Raven and how he brought the sun to the world. So Cicely is decorated with ravens in every possible form. I chip in by making this black bread. Joel Fleischman took one look at it and called it pumpernickel, which it is not.

Still, it goes well with cream cheese.

Cornmeal to dust baking sheet
1 large egg, at room temperature
1 cup buttermilk
¼ cup dark molasses
2 teaspoons instant coffee granules
2 tablespoons vegetable oil
1½ cups all-purpose flour
1½ cups rye flour, preferably stone-ground
½ tablespoon baking powder
1 teaspoon baking soda
1 teaspoon salt

> **"THERE'S NOTHING LIKE THE SIGHT OF A BEAUTIFUL, BLACK-AS-PITCH RAVEN TO FILL YOU WITH THE CHRISTMAS SPIRIT."**
> **—CHRIS STEVENS**

1 ◆ Preheat oven to 375°F. Lightly grease a baking sheet and dust with cornmeal.

2 ◆ In a large bowl, beat egg with an electric mixer. Add buttermilk, molasses, coffee granules, and vegetable oil one at a time, mixing well after each addition.

3 ◆ Combine flours, baking powder, baking soda, and salt and sift into the liquid mixture. Stir well with a wooden spoon.

4 ◆ Dust hands with flour and knead dough lightly for about 30 seconds, working in all the flour. Form into a ball and then flatten somewhat to create a round loaf that is approximately 8 inches across. Place on prepared baking sheet.

5 ◆ Lightly dust the top of loaf with flour. Using a very sharp knife that has been dipped in flour, cut a shallow X across most of the top. Bake for 40 to 45 minutes, until bread sounds hollow when lightly tapped on bottom.

MAKES 1 LOAF

DAVE'S EGGNOG

You wouldn't think Dave would have a special skill at making something like eggnog. But isn't it interesting that he does? That happens a lot, doesn't it? You see football players who knit, truck drivers who build ships in a bottle. . . . Maybe it's not as interesting as I thought.

The heat has to be low, or you'll get scrambled eggs. I say, don't use dark rum, because it'll clash with the brandy. Somebody said, where's the nutmeg? Do what you want.

But just because you serve it in a glass doesn't mean it's a drink. It's more like a dessert or a food. I put this out, Holling says, Well, what shall we put out with it? I say, What do you mean? He says, We want to serve alcoholic beverages with some kind of accompaniment, like nuts or minipretzels. I say, Accompany it with *nothing*. With a napkin.

Do what you want.

6 *large eggs, separated*
8 *cups light cream*
1 *cup granulated sugar*
1 *tablespoon vanilla extract*
2 *cups brandy*
1 *cup light rum*
½ *cup confectioners' sugar*

1 ◆ Put egg yolks and 6 cups of the cream into a heavy saucepan. Cook over very low heat, stirring constantly, until mixture is thick enough to coat the back of a spoon. Remove from heat and set aside.

2 ◆ In a large bowl, combine granulated sugar, vanilla extract, brandy, and rum. Beat in egg yolk mixture until well combined.

3 ◆ In the top of a double boiler, over boiling water, beat egg whites to soft peaks with an electric mixer. Gradu-

> "THE CHRISTMAS TREE IS A MAJOR CHRISTIAN SYMBOL. I MEAN, NEXT TO THE CROSS ITSELF, YOU CAN'T GET ANYTHING THAT'S MORE CHRISTIAN. TRADITIONALLY, JEWS AVOID CHRISTIAN SYMBOLS.
> NOT THAT I HAVEN'T FANTASIZED ABOUT HAVING A TREE . . . AND IT IS TRUE THAT I ENJOY, EVEN EMBRACE, OTHER TRAPPINGS OF THE HOLIDAY SEASON—THE MUSIC, THE GIFT GIVING. I MEAN, YOU DON'T HAVE TO BE A REPUBLICAN TO CELEBRATE LINCOLN'S BIRTHDAY."
> —JOEL FLEISCHMAN

ally add confectioners' sugar, continuing to beat until stiff peaks are formed.

4 ♦ Gently stir beaten egg whites and the remaining 2 cups cream into egg yolk mixture.

5 ♦ Cover and refrigerate until ready to serve.

MAKES ABOUT 14 CUPS

MAGGIE ON THE MANY QUESTIONS OF CHRISTMAS

I used to cringe every Christmastime when my parents would send me an airline ticket to spend the holiday with them back home. Now they're divorced. No tickets, no going home, no cringing. Instead: guilt.

Is either of them devastated, having to endure the holiday season without each other? Or without me or my brother? If the answer (assuming I were ever actually to hear it) were No, then the *next* question is, Should they therefore have gotten divorced sooner? Did they stay together in misery and recrimination because of me and my brother? Should I feel guilty about that?

And if the answer is Yes, then should I in fact fly home to console one? The other? Both? And, since I have no intention of flying anywhere, should I feel guilty about that?

Just a few personal thoughts for the holiday season.

OLD-FASHIONED PLUM PUDDING WITH HARD SAUCE

1½ cups golden raisins
1 cup dried currants
½ cup chopped dried figs
2 tablespoons chopped candied orange peel
¼ cup chopped candied citron
¾ cup finely chopped suet
2 cups bread crumbs
2 teaspoons ground cinnamon
1 teaspoon ground ginger
½ teaspoon ground nutmeg
¼ teaspoon ground cloves
¼ teaspoon ground mace
½ teaspoon salt
1 cup sugar
4 large eggs
3 tablespoons milk
6 tablespoons brandy
6 tablespoons white vermouth
1 cup Hard Sauce (recipe follows)

> "AS A KID—AND LET'S FACE IT, KIDS LOOK AT THESE HOLIDAYS MATERIALISTICALLY—I ALWAYS THOUGHT HANUKKAH WAS A BETTER DEAL. EIGHT PRESENTS, RIGHT? AND THEY'RE STAGGERED OVER A WEEK SO YOU'RE FORCED TO SAVOR EACH ONE. WITH CHRISTMAS, YOU GET EVERYTHING ALL AT ONCE. IT'S EASY TO OVERLOAD."
> —JOEL FLEISCHMAN

1 ♦ Grease a 2-quart pudding mold or casserole. Put a rack in the bottom of a large pot. Fill the pot with enough water to come halfway up the sides of the mold or casserole when placed on the rack. Bring water to boil.

2 ♦ Combine raisins, currants, figs, candied orange peel and citron, suet, bread crumbs, spices, salt, and sugar in a large bowl. Mix thoroughly.

3 ♦ In another bowl, beat eggs until foamy, using an electric mixer. Beat in milk, brandy, and vermouth. Fold into fruit mixture until well blended.

4 ♦ Pour batter into pudding mold and secure top. (If using a casserole dish, cover with a double thickness of aluminum foil tied securely with string.) Place mold on rack in boiling water. Cover the pot and lower heat. Gently boil for 5 hours. Check periodically and add more water as needed to maintain a depth of about halfway up the sides of the mold or casserole.

5 ♦ Remove pudding from pot and let cool for 10 minutes before unmolding. Serve while still warm, with Hard Sauce on the side.

MAKES 8–12 SERVINGS

HARD SAUCE

⅓ *cup unsalted butter, at room*
  temperature
¾ *teaspoon vanilla extract*
1 cup confectioners' sugar

1 ♦ In a small bowl, cream butter with an electric mixer until light and fluffy. Add vanilla extract and sugar gradually while beating. Continue beating until smooth and creamy. Serve with plum pudding.

MAKES ABOUT 1 CUP

MAURICE ON CHRISTMAS TRADITION

I am not a religious man, but I respect the traditions of Christmas, with one pointed exception. We're talking about celebrating a birth that occurred roughly two thousand years ago. That gives us twenty centuries of gastronomic history from which to draw inspiration.

Then will someone please tell me why the hell our notion of a "traditional" Christmas celebration is dominated by the fulsome fantasies of a nineteenth-century British novelist? I admire Dickens as much as the next man, but you're talking about a person heir to a culinary tradition of *no* culinary tradition. Roast beef, Yorkshire pudding, roast goose: fine dishes, occasionally, but not the sort of thing I would base a major annual feast around.

Christianity is a world religion spanning millennia. Can't we do better, people?

JOEL'S OVEN-ROASTED CHESTNUTS

This is not the most sophisticated recipe in the world, but it is evocative. And coming from Joel, it means so much, doesn't it?

Yes, New York is a very Jewish city, but that doesn't mean we don't have colorfully Dickensian chestnut vendors on the street come December. We do. (We also have dreadfully Dickensian homeless people, but that's another story.) So despite what some readers may think, I actually do have firsthand, real-life chestnut-eating experience.

Roasting experience, too. I actually made this. Once.

3 pounds fresh chestnuts

1 ◆ Preheat oven to 500°F.

2 ◆ Using a sharp knife, cut an X across the top of each chestnut shell. Place cut chestnuts on a baking sheet and cook for 15 minutes, until the X has curled open and the exposed meat looks golden. Serve.

MAKES 8-14 SERVINGS

> "ACTUALLY, YOU KNOW, I'VE ALWAYS LIKED CHRISTMAS. IT'S A GREAT HOLIDAY FOR JEWISH KIDS—TWO WEEKS OUT OF SCHOOL AND NOTHING'S EXPECTED OF YOU."
> —JOEL FLEISCHMAN

MATZO BALL SOUP

6 large eggs, separated
½ teaspoon kosher salt
⅛ teaspoon freshly ground black pepper
2 tablespoons unsalted butter, melted
1 cup matzo meal
Bubbe Fleischman's Chicken Soup
   (see Index)

> "YOU KNOW, I TRIED. I GAVE IT A REAL GOOD SHOT. BUT IT JUST DIDN'T WORK. SCRATCH THE PLUM PUDDING, THERE'S A MATZO BALL UNDERNEATH. I'M A JEW—THAT'S ALL THERE IS TO IT."
>
> —JOEL FLEISCHMAN

1 ♦ Whisk egg yolks until light and fluffy. While continuing to whisk, add salt, pepper, and butter.

2 ♦ In a large bowl, beat egg whites until stiff peaks are formed. Fold into egg yolk mixture. Fold in matzo meal, a little at a time, until all is incorporated. Cover and refrigerate for at least 1 hour.

3 ♦ When ready to cook, bring a large pot of water to a boil. Remove batter from refrigerator. With damp hands, roll a heaping tablespoonful at a time between palms of hands to form dough balls the size of a golf ball. When all the batter has been formed into balls, drop balls into the boiling water. Lower heat to simmer, cover pot, and cook for 30 minutes. Remove matzo balls from water and drain.

4 ♦ Serve with Bubbe Fleischman's Chicken Soup.

MAKES 10-12 SERVINGS

🫎 11 🫎

A RUSSIAN FEAST

NOW THAT RUSSIA'S NO LONGER THE ENEMY,
THINGS ARE NOT AS INTERESTING AS THEY
USED TO BE. BUT THAT'S THE FATE OF THE
ARMED SERVICES, ISN'T IT—TO MAKE LIFE
INCREASINGLY DULL.

— MAURICE MINNIFIELD

THE BRICK'S BORSCHT

Holling makes this once a year, when Nikolai Appolanov, the Russian musician, drops by.

I don't know why I don't make this more often. It's great cold, and when it comes to really substantial cold soups, it's a lot easier finding decent beets than decent tomatoes for something like gazpacho.

10 red beets, peeled and shredded	*1 teaspoon salt*
2 carrots, peeled, trimmed, and shredded	*4 teaspoons sugar*
1 white onion, peeled and grated	*2 tablespoons lemon juice*
8 cups water	*½ cup sour cream*

1 ◆ Combine beets, carrots, onion, water, and salt in a large saucepan. Bring to a boil over medium heat. Cook for 30 minutes.

2 ◆ Stir in sugar and lemon juice. Cook for an additional 5 minutes.

3 ◆ Ladle into 8 soup bowls and garnish with sour cream.

MAKES 8 SERVINGS

JOEL ON THE RUSSIAN FEAST

I don't understand the compulsion to entertain someone from another culture by providing for them the food or diversions of the very culture they just came from. Why does Cicely put out this enormous Russian spread when Nikolai Appolanov comes to town? Hasn't he come here to get away from Russia? Doesn't he, or his wife, or his domestic staff, or whoever, do kasha and pirozhki *better* than Holling or Dave? Shouldn't they be serving him shrimp creole or barbecued ribs or fried chicken?

Don't misunderstand, I agree with the basic idea, which is to honor your guest. But when I go to Italy—which I definitely will, some day—I don't want to be welcomed with second-rate hot dogs. I want Italian!

PIROZHKI

Nikolai brings these, which are little Russian meat pies. The introduction is from Dave, who occasionally makes pirozhki in the off-season.

I like the idea of these little pies. I make them once in a while at The Brick. You can put stuff inside and seal it up. Food that holds and protects other food seems like an advanced thing to me.

DOUGH
1½ cups all-purpose flour
½ teaspoon salt
½ teaspoon baking powder
½ cup (1 stick) unsalted butter
3 tablespoons cold water

FILLING
2 tablespoons vegetable oil
1 white onion, peeled and finely chopped
1 pound ground chuck

1 ◆ Preheat oven to 425°F. Lightly grease a cookie sheet.

2 ◆ Sift flour, salt, and baking powder together into a bowl. Using a fork, cut in butter to form a coarse meal. Add water and mix together to form a dough ball. Set aside.

3 ◆ To make filling, heat oil over medium heat in a heavy skillet. Add onion and sauté until wilted (about 5 minutes). Add meat and cook until browned (about 6 or 7 minutes), breaking up the meat as it cooks. Remove from heat.

4 ◆ Place dough ball onto a floured surface and roll out to a ¼ inch thickness. Cut dough into 3-inch squares.

5 ◆ Place 1 teaspoon of filling in the center of each square. Fold one corner of the dough over to form a triangle. With the tines of a fork, press down along the outer edges to seal.

6 ◆ Place filled, sealed pirozhki on the prepared cookie sheet and bake until golden brown (about 15 minutes).

MAKES ABOUT 30 PIROZHKI

ROAST CHICKEN

1½ cups warm mashed cooked potatoes
¾ cup (1½ sticks) unsalted butter, melted
2 cups bread crumbs
1½ cups coarsely chopped white
*   mushrooms*
2 tablespoons chopped fresh parsley
2 tablespoons chopped fresh basil
2 tablespoons chopped fresh chives
½ teaspoon salt
¼ teaspoon freshly ground black pepper
1 4-pound roasting chicken, well rinsed
¼ cup olive oil

1 ◆ Preheat oven to 350°F.

2 ◆ Mix potatoes and butter in a large bowl until butter is completely absorbed. Add all remaining ingredients except chicken and oil and mix thoroughly.

3 ◆ Loosely stuff potato mixture into cavity of the chicken.

4 ◆ Rub chicken all over with olive oil. Place on a rack in a roasting pan that has been lined with aluminum foil. Roast for 2 hours, 15 minutes, until juices run clear when chicken is pricked with a fork.

MAKES 8–10 SERVINGS

RUSSIAN POT ROAST

1 7-pound beef brisket
½ teaspoon kosher salt
¼ teaspoon ground black pepper
1 tablespoon vegetable oil
2 white onions, peeled and thinly sliced
2 carrots, peeled, trimmed, and sliced
    in rounds
2 ribs celery, sliced
2 tomatoes, coarsely chopped
2 cloves garlic, peeled and thinly sliced
1 cup dry red wine

1 ◆ Salt and pepper brisket.

2 ◆ Heat oil in a Dutch oven. Place brisket into hot oil, fatty side down, and cook over high heat for 5 minutes to brown. Add all remaining ingredients. Cover, lower heat, and simmer for 3 hours, until meat is fork-tender.

MAKES 8–12 SERVINGS

TODAY'S SPECIAL

Chicken Kiev special
Stroganoff no peas.

◆

MAGGIE ON JOEL ON THE RUSSIAN FEAST

Ruth-Anne showed me Fleischman's comment about our Russian banquet for Nikolai and, as usual, Fleischman has missed the point completely. The purpose of the feast is not to "expose" Nikolai to food he needs no exposure to. The point—are you reading this, Fleischman?—is to *honor* him by doing tribute to his native cuisine. Fleischman, who, with the provinciality of the typical New Yorker, assumes the entire world exists as a theme park for his entertainment, for "broadening" his own petty ego, assumes that the point of travel is to collect as many "experiences" as you can. Someone should tell him that Nikolai comes here not to have an "experience" but to visit friends.

KASHA

¼ *cup (½ stick) unsalted butter*
1 white onion, peeled and finely chopped
1½ cups buckwheat groats
4 cups milk
1½ teaspoons salt

1 ◆ Melt butter in a heavy saucepan. Add onion and sauté over medium heat until wilted (about 5 minutes).

2 ◆ Add groats to onions. Mix until groats are well coated with butter. Add milk and salt. Cover, lower heat, and simmer for 30 minutes, until all liquid is absorbed and groats are tender.

MAKES 8–12 SERVINGS

BOILED POTATOES

24 small new red potatoes, peeled
5 tablespoons unsalted butter
1 white onion, peeled and finely chopped
2 teaspoons caraway seeds

1 ♦ Put potatoes into a saucepan and cover with water. Bring to a boil, and boil for about 15 minutes, until potatoes are fork-tender. Remove from heat and drain.

2 ♦ While potatoes are still hot, transfer to a serving bowl. Add remaining ingredients and toss to mix until butter has melted.

MAKES 8–12 SERVINGS

HOLLING ON THE END OF THE COLD WAR

Now that the Cold War is over, when Nikolai pays his annual visit I notice there's much less of a buzz in The Brick. Before it used to feel like we were all striking a blow for world peace just by being seen in public with him, even if we were only being seen by one another. Now it feels like a call by a poor relation. Not that we don't admire him personally, of course.

 12 🐄

POTLUCK FARE

POTLUCK—YOU MIGHT THINK IT IMPLIES LUCK
THAT'S GONE TO POT. BUT IT'S REALLY
COOKING'S ALL-STAR GAME. AND, AS WITH
ANY ALL-STAR GAME, IT'S LESS A MATTER OF
COMPETITION THAN A DISPLAY OF PROWESS.
I'LL TAKE POTLUCK ANYTIME.

— CHRIS STEVENS

MONKS' CASSOULET

Chris brought this recipe back from—of all places—a monastery. Well, I say of all places, but monks have to eat, too, I suppose. Still, something this good from a place devoted to renunciation does strike me as a bit surprising.

What I learned at the monastery, people, is that a monastery is no place for me. Something in me—psyche, soul, animus, call it what you will—malfunctions in the absence of women. It was a chastening lesson, since until then I had fancied that spiritually I was "above" the relatively crude demands of gender polarity. Even the fine work of the monastery kitchen (of which this is an example) wasn't enough to make up for a lack of open proximity to the female sex. So what did a spiritual retreat contribute to yours truly? That insight, plus a great bean dish—maybe not a profound spiritual revelation, but not a bad week's work.

2 cups dried Great Northern beans
8 cups chicken stock
2 tablespoons vegetable oil
1 pound white onions, peeled and coarsely
      chopped
3 cloves garlic, peeled and finely chopped
1½ pounds tomatoes, seeded and coarsely
      chopped
10 sprigs parsley
2 teaspoons dried thyme
4 bay leaves
10 whole black peppercorns
¼ cup virgin olive oil
1 4–5 pound duck, cut into 10 pieces
2 pounds boneless lamb shoulder, cut into
      2-inch cubes
1½ pounds boneless pork shoulder, cut into
      2-inch cubes
2 cups dry white wine
1 pound Toulouse sausage
½ pound slab bacon

1 ◆ Wash beans in cold water and drain. Combine beans and chicken stock in an ovenproof 8-quart casserole. Bring to a boil over high heat and continue to boil for 10 minutes. Remove the pot from heat and set aside.

2 ◆ Preheat oven to 350°F.

3 ◆ Heat vegetable oil in a frying pan over low heat. Add onions and sauté until tender (about 15 minutes). Add garlic and tomatoes and continue to sauté for about 20 minutes, until all liquid has evaporated. Pour into the bean pot and stir well.

4 ◆ Create a bouquet garni by placing parsley, thyme, bay leaves, and peppercorns into a 6-inch square double thickness of cheesecloth, gathering the ends together, and tying securely closed with string. Add to the bean pot.

5 ◆ Cover beans, place the pot in the oven, and bake for 2 hours.

6 ◆ While beans are baking, heat olive oil over medium heat in a large frying pan. In small batches, brown duck, lamb, and pork in the hot oil. As meat is browned, transfer it to a large bowl, using a slotted spoon.

7 ◆ When beans have baked for 2 hours, empty the bowl of browned meat, along with any juices that have collected, into the bean pot. Add wine, stir thoroughly, cover the pot, and bake for another 2 hours.

8 ◆ Fill a saucepan half-full with water and bring to a boil over high heat. Prick the skin of the sausage all over with a fork and place in the boiling water. Lower heat and simmer for 40 minutes. Drain and set sausage aside to cool.

9 ◆ Put bacon into a saucepan, cover with cold water, and bring to a boil over high heat. Lower heat and simmer for 15 minutes. Drain, cover bacon with cold water, and repeat process. Drain again and set aside.

10 ◆ Discard casing from cooled sausage. Cut sausage into rounds. Cut bacon into small cubes.

11 ◆ When beans have baked for a total of 4 hours, remove the pot from the oven. Stir in sausage and bacon. Return to oven and bake, uncovered, for 45 minutes more.

MAKES 12 SERVINGS

GREEN BEAN CASSEROLE

A contribution from Maggie and Mike Monroe. I asked Maggie to explain it and, you know, for a second she couldn't even <u>recall</u> it. Maybe there's a reason for that and maybe there isn't.

Ruth-Anne asked me for this recipe after Mike left. We had made it when Marilyn's Raven clan celebrated the unveiling of their totem pole, which generated a rift between her clan and the Bear clan. First the clans had a falling out; then, a little while later, Mike left. Not that one had anything to do with the other. I mean, if you serve this to a group of twelve, they won't all start fighting or leave you forever. Probably.

2 cups chicken broth
½ cup finely chopped white onion
½ cup heavy cream
½ teaspoon white pepper
¼ teaspoon salt
1 tablespoon cornstarch
¼ cup milk
1 cup thinly sliced fresh mushrooms
2½ pounds fresh green beans, washed and
    trimmed
¼ cup dry sherry
½ cup slivered blanched almonds

1 ◆ Place broth and onion in a medium-sized saucepan and bring to a rolling boil. Reduce heat to medium and cook for 20 minutes. Reduce heat to low and add cream, pepper, and salt.

2 ◆ Preheat oven to 350°F.

3 ◆ In a small cup, thoroughly mix together cornstarch and milk. Slowly add cornstarch mixture to sauce, stirring constantly with a wire whisk until sauce is thick and creamy. Add mushrooms and simmer over very low heat.

4 ◆ While sauce is simmering, steam green beans until tender (about 10 minutes). Transfer beans to a casserole dish.

5 ◆ Stir sherry into sauce and pour evenly over green beans. Top with almonds and bake for 20 minutes. Serve.

MAKES 12 SERVINGS

RUTH-ANNE'S LASAGNA

2 tablespoons vegetable oil
1 white onion, peeled and chopped
1 rib celery, chopped
1 clove garlic, peeled and chopped
½ pound ground beef
1 28-ounce can Italian tomatoes
1 6-ounce can tomato paste
1 tablespoon dried oregano
1 tablespoon dried basil
½ teaspoon salt
¼ teaspoon ground black pepper
1 tablespoon sugar
1½ cups ricotta cheese
1 large egg
½ pound lasagna noodles, cooked according
*   to package directions*
¾ cup shredded mozzarella cheese

1 ◆ Preheat oven to 350°F. Lightly grease a 13″ × 10″ × 2″ baking pan.

2 ◆ Heat oil in a large frying pan. Add onion, celery, and garlic and sauté over medium heat, until onion has wilted (about 5 minutes). Add beef and cook for 5 minutes to brown. Add tomatoes and their juice, tomato paste, oregano, basil, salt, pepper, and sugar. Bring to a boil. Lower heat and simmer, uncovered, for 20 minutes, stirring occasionally.

3 ◆ In a small bowl, mix together ricotta cheese and egg.

4 ◆ Line the bottom of the prepared baking pan with a layer of noodles placed lengthwise. Top with a layer of sauce. Over the sauce, add a layer of the ricotta-egg mixture. Sprinkle a layer of mozzarella cheese on top. Repeat entire layering process two more times, ending with a top layer of mozzarella cheese.

5 ◆ Bake for 25 minutes, until top is golden brown.

MAKES 8–10 SERVINGS

MAGGIE'S LASAGNA

3 tablespoons virgin olive oil
1 zucchini, cut into thin strips
1 yellow squash, cut into thin strips
1 green bell pepper, cored, seeded, and cut
    into thin strips
1 red bell pepper, cored, seeded, and cut
    into thin strips
1 yellow bell pepper, cored, seeded, and cut
    into thin strips
1 large yellow onion, peeled and thinly
    sliced
8 ounces white button mushrooms, sliced
1 8-ounce package lasagna noodles
5 tablespoons unsalted butter
¼ cup all-purpose flour
2 cups milk
⅛ teaspoon white pepper
5 tablespoons grated Parmesan
½ cup chopped fresh basil
12 ounces mozzarella cheese, grated

1 ◆ Preheat oven to 375°F.

2 ◆ Heat 2 tablespoons of the oil in a large frying pan over medium heat. Add zucchini, yellow squash, bell peppers, and onion. Cook until onion is translucent (about 6 minutes). Do not allow vegetables to brown. Transfer vegetables to a bowl with a slotted spoon.

3 ◆ Add the remaining tablespoon of oil and mushrooms to the frying pan. Sauté for 5 minutes, until wilted. Remove mushrooms with a slotted spoon and combine with the other cooked vegetables.

4 ◆ Fill a 3-quart saucepan about halfway with water and bring to a boil. Add noodles and cook just until tender (about 8 minutes). Put noodles in a colander, rinse under cold running water, and drain.

5 ◆ In a heavy-bottomed saucepan, melt butter over low heat. Stir in flour with a wire whisk and cook for 3 minutes, whisking constantly to a smooth consistency.

6 ◆ Raise heat to medium and slowly add milk while whisking, continuing to whisk until sauce thickens. Remove from heat and whisk in white pepper and Parmesan. Spread a small amount of the sauce over the bottom of a 13″ × 10″ × 2″ baking dish.

7 ◆ Arrange one-third of the noodles, lengthwise, over the sauce and cover with half of the vegetables. Top with one-third of the remaining sauce and one-third of the basil and mozzarella. Layer another third of the noodles, cover with the remaining vegetables, and top with another third of the sauce, basil, and mozzarella. Layer the last third of the noodles on top and cover with the last third of the sauce, basil, and mozzarella. Cover with aluminum foil.

8 ◆ Bake for 20 minutes, remove the foil, and bake for an additional 10 minutes, until the top has browned.

MAKES 8–12 SERVINGS

SHELLY'S LASAGNA

1 8-ounce package medium egg noodles,
    cooked per package directions and
    drained
1 white onion, peeled and chopped
1 green bell pepper, chopped
1 cup sour cream
1 cup cottage cheese

2 tablespoons olive oil
1 pound ground chuck
½ teaspoon salt
½ teaspoon ground black pepper
½ teaspoon garlic powder
1 6-ounce can tomato sauce
½ cup shredded mozzarella cheese

1 ♦ Preheat oven to 325°F. Lightly grease a 2-quart casserole dish.

2 ♦ In a large bowl, mix together noodles, onion, green pepper, sour cream, and cottage cheese. Set aside.

3 ♦ In a heavy frying pan, heat oil over medium heat. Add ground chuck and cook for about 5 minutes, stirring constantly, until browned. Pour off and discard any fat remaining in the pan and return the pan to the heat. Add salt, pepper, garlic powder, and tomato sauce. Reduce heat and simmer for 5 minutes.

4 ♦ Fill the casserole with alternating layers of noodle mixture and meat, beginning with noodles and ending with meat. Sprinkle cheese over top.

5 ♦ Bake for 25 minutes, until cheese has melted and browned.

MAKES 8–12 SERVINGS

MAGGIE ON LASAGNAMANIA

What we're talking about here is noodles and accompaniment, really. It could feature meat or in my case, be vegetarian. But the idea is universal. The Japanese serve noodles in broth with meat; the Greeks make pastitsio. Even the Americans serve chili with macaroni—OK, they mainly do that in Cincinnati, but that counts.

Everybody makes lasagna for our annual spring Meltdown feast, probably for the same reason I do: by the time Meltdown arrives, I get so crazed and pent-up I forget all the other dishes I had vowed to make instead and just fall back on the old standby. Still, no one complains. No, wait, that's not quite true. Fleischman complained, didn't he? Ask me if I'm surprised.

JOEL'S JELL-O SUPREME

I wanted to call this "Joel's Jell-O," but Joel took offense. He said that name would demean his contribution. I said if tacking the word "supreme" onto the end of things would mean the difference between his feeling demeaned and not demeaned, it was fine with me.

Jell-O. An American institution. Say what you will about its nutritional shortcomings—which by the way are addressed here by the addition of fresh bananas—Jell-O is synonymous with fun in an edible form.

I made this on the occasion of my first Meltdown. (I remember the occasion well, since it was highlighted by O'Connell and me going temporarily insane and finding ourselves in a passionate embrace that destroyed half of Holling's kitchen.) But before that, O'Connell gave me grief about adding the bananas after the Jell-O had set. So I have corrected the recipe accordingly. The next time O'Connell tells you I'm arrogant and unwilling to learn from others, just show her this.

4 3-ounce boxes strawberry flavored
    Jell-O
4 ripe bananas

1 ♦ Prepare Jell-O according to package directions (I recommend the quick-set method, with the ice cubes). Let chill in a serving bowl.

2 ♦ When Jell-O has set about halfway (so that it's thick enough to suspend fruit), slice bananas and mix into Jell-O. Let chill until thoroughly set. Serve.

MAKES 8–12 SERVINGS

MAURICE ON COOKBOOKS

A good cookbook is like an atlas. Each recipe is a map. It gets you pointed in the right direction, but it's up to you to find your way through a dish once you get oriented. I don't want to make too much of what is admittedly a fairly uninspired analogy, but the point is, cooking is neither an art nor a science. It's a craft. You learn some technique, you use common sense, and you allow for occasional flashes of inspiration.

But don't talk to me about cooking as some means of "self-expression." Most people's selves can't bear much expressing, and I'm not so sure I want to be there to eat the result when it happens.

ᴖ EPISODE REFERENCE ᴖ GUIDE

1 TODAY'S BREAKFAST SPECIAL

Griddle Cakes: ("A Kodiak Moment," 1990) Life, death, and family are examined as Maurice loses his brother and auditions Chris for the role of adopted son and heir to the Minnifield empire. (Chris: "It's six-fifteen, chinooks. Rise and shine. I can smell those griddle cakes. Mom's squeezing the Valencias. Dad's getting ready for work. Today is family day here on Chris-in-the-Morning.")

Adam's German Apple Pancake: ("Dateline: Cicely," 1992) Adam commandeers the kitchen at The Brick while working as an anonymous reporter for Maurice's *Cicely News and World Telegram.* (Joel: "Is that the German apple pancake?")

The Brick's House Omelette: ("Roots," 1991) After sampling the fare (Adam: "Is this supposed to be a mushroom? This isn't a meal—it's Twenty Questions. Shoelace? Color swatch? Surely you don't call this a tomato."), Adam makes a wager with Holling that he can create better cuisine. (Adam: "In 48 hours, I'd have people lined up outside *begging* to be let in.")

Denver Omelette: ("The Bad Seed," 1992) Marilyn feels the need for a place of her own when living under her mother's roof—and rules—becomes frustrating. (Marilyn: "Denver today." Marilyn's mom: "I had ham.")

Devil's Mess Eggs: ("Animals R Us," 1991) Maggie's dead boyfriend Rick returns, finicky eating habits intact, as a dog. (Maggie: "Devil's mess eggs, that OK with you, boy? . . . You left the green peppers. Why? *Rick* didn't like green peppers . . .")

Adam's Eggs Florentine: ("Dateline: Cicely," 1992) Adam cooks up a storm while

161

working undercover for Maurice's local paper. (Joel: "Wait, wait, wait! Hold it right there. What is that?" Shelly: "Uh, this is eggs florentine . . .")

Cheese Blintzes with Blueberry Sauce: ("Dateline: Cicely," 1992) Adam again, working hard to prove that pots and pans belong in the hands of trained professionals, attempts to teach Dave how to cook. (Adam: "No, no, no! You want to drown it? It has to breathe, to float! . . . You're not ready for crepes, Dave. Go boil some water.")

Biscuits and Gravy: ("Three Amigos," 1992) Maurice and Holling's hunting friend dies, and the two set off to bury him at a remote spot in the Alaskan wilderness. The friend's widow, Solvang, accompanies the men and treats them to a hearty breakfast. (Maurice: "I've got to say, these are some of the best biscuits I've ever tasted." Holling: "Gravy, too. Smooth as silk." Solvang: "I love to watch a man eat. More squirrel?")

2 APPETIZERS

Adam's Walnut Toast with Warm Goat Cheese: ("Dateline: Cicely," 1992) Another culinary delight from Adam at The Brick. (Shelly: "Your walnut toast with hot goat cheese will be up in a minute, Dr. Fleischman." Joel: "Thanks, Shelly. I think I'll have it over there, away from Medusa, if you don't mind.")

Diego's Maíz Azul Supreme: ("Dateline: Cicely," 1992) Adam reminisces about a dead comrade as everyone else rhapsodizes over Adam's mini tacos. (Shelly: I don't know what you call 'em, but I've been scarfing 'em down like beer nuts.")

Adam's Pot Stickers: ("The Bumpy Road to Love," 1991) An irate Joel is held hostage as a captive doctor-on-call at Adam and Eve's cabin. (Joel: "Do you realize the humiliation you caused me last year? Nobody believed me. I'm telling them, yeah, I saw Adam, Cicely's own bigfoot—Mr. Sasquatch. He cooked me pot stickers and Szechwan chicken in a wok in the middle of nowhere.")

Maurice's Spicy Chicken Wings: ("Goodbye to All That," 1991) Maurice wonders whether Chris is upset at having to take up residence at the station after his trailer is destroyed. (Maurice: "Chris isn't all bent out of shape about this housing thing, is he? . . . Last night, I made up a batch of those spicy chicken wings he likes. He didn't come, he didn't call.")

3 SALADS

The Brick's Caesar Salad: ("Ill Wind," 1992) Joel and Maggie hit the hay—literally—as passion finally overcomes mutual irritation. Afterward, they stop by The Brick to grab a bite and share the news. (Maggie: "Wanna split a Caesar's?" Joel: "Yeah, sure.")

Maurice's Greens with Balsamic Vinaigrette: ("Slow Dance," 1991) Maurice questions his manhood when he realizes that Erick and Ron, prospective home buyers who share his love for Broadway musicals and gourmet food, are homosexual. (Erick: "Maurice, do you have any balsamic vinegar?" Maurice: "Cupboard to your right.")

Potato Salad: ("Slow Dance," 1991) At Rick's funeral, Chris reviews the various ways in which Maggie's boyfriends met their maker. (Chris: "A lot of you know about Rick's predecessor, Dave, who fell asleep on a glacier and froze to death. But before Dave, there was Glen—he and his Volvo took a wrong turn and ended up on a missile test range. Then there was Bruce—the victim of a freak croquet accident. And before him, Harry—he died . . . how was it? . . . That's right—the potato salad.")

Mea Culpa Three-Bean Salad: ("Jules et Joel," 1991) KBHR broadcasts a call-in radio program that encourages folks to reach out and confess. (Chris: "Yes, ma'am, what's gnawing at your conscience?" Caller: "Well, last night I had a few friends over for dinner and I made my three-bean salad which everyone likes so much. . . . The thing is, I opened the can of red beans and it didn't smell right. But you know, I just hate to waste. . . . And this morning . . . well, usually my friends call to thank me for a lovely evening—but so far, I haven't heard from a one." Chris: "Hmmm. Well, I wouldn't be too hard on myself—there's always a certain amount of risk in eating out. That's the trade-off for not having to do the dishes. OK. Next caller. You're on the air.")

Maurice's Coleslaw: ("What I Did for Love," 1991) Maurice continues a longtime clandestine affair with a married woman. Raiding the refrigerator, the two share a late-night snack of cold chicken and coleslaw.

Warm Duck Salad with Fennel: ("Roots," 1991) Adam's in The Brick's kitchen, making good on his wager with Holling that he can produce incredible edibles behind the counter. (Chris: "And the warm duck salad, incredible. There's something in here—" Adam: "Yeah, yeah. Fennel, OK?")

Shelly's Ambrosia Salad: ("The Bad Seed," 1992) Shelly is miffed at Holling when she discovers that he'd thought he was sterile and hadn't told her, but with a few kind words about her culinary skills and some heartfelt groveling, Holling wins her over. (Shelly: "I hope I didn't put in too many marshmallows again this time." Holling: "Oh no no no. Your ambrosia salads are one of the most popular items on the menu, Shelly. Many customers on several occasions have commented to me of their appreciation of your fine salads.")

4 SOUPS AND STEWS

Bubbe Fleischman's Chicken Soup: ("The Russian Flu," 1990) Cicely is hit with a flu epidemic. (Joel: "Outside of plenty of rest and my bubbe's recipe for chicken soup, all we can do is let the virus run its course.")

Marilyn's Fresh Turnip Soup: ("Get Real," 1991) Cicely enjoys the arrival of the circus and Marilyn brings Enrico Bellati, the lovestruck Flying Man, home for dinner. (Marilyn: "Good soup, Mom." Marilyn's mom: "Fresh turnips.")

Adam's Lamb Stew: ("Roots," 1991) Adam puts in more time behind the counter at The Brick. (Maggie: "Can you believe this food? I just had a lamb stew that was—I mean, I've had lamb stew before, plenty of times, we all have, right? But this—from now on, when I think of lamb stew . . .")

The Brick's Kick-Ass Chili: ("Dateline: Cicely," 1992) In return for Chris's loaning him some much-needed money, Holling makes Chris a partner in The Brick. Unfortunately, this causes the normally philosophical deejay to start obsessing about things like coasters and "the bottom line." (Chris: "All I'm saying is that Leon's Roadhouse in Sweetwater charges three-fifty for a bowl of chili half this size—and theirs comes out of a can.")

Maggie's Gumbo: ("Spring Break," 1991) As the town waits for the annual ice melt-down, spring fever has everyone acting a bit out of character. (Shelly: "What are you making?" Maggie: "Gumbo. I really need okra—the zucchini'll just have to do. . . . Carrots . . . zucchini . . . onions . . ." Shelly: "I thought you hated to cook." Maggie: "Shelly, people change. People grow. Celery! . . . You don't have any filé. Never mind. I'll use cumin.")

5 ENTREES

The Brick's Tuna Supreme: ("Aurora Borealis," 1990) Alternately called a tuna melt in other episodes, this is a popular dish at The Brick. (Shelly: "Who had the Tuna Supreme?")

Dave's Salmon Steaks: ("Jules et Joel," 1991) Fleischman's twin brother Jules very convincingly pretends to be Joel, as the two sample the catch of the day at The Brick. (Joel: "Tell the chef, the *proper* way to prepare salmon is to poach or steam it only 'til it turns a lighter shade of pink.")

Salmon Loaf: ("Only You," 1991) Maurice and Holling's feud over Shelly heats up again. (Holling: "Joel, I remember every detail of the day he brought Shelly to Cicely. It was Tuesday—I'd had a good lunch crowd—ran out of the Salmon Loaf. . . .")

Maurice's Poached Salmon: ("Animals R Us," 1991) Maurice gets into the ostrich-egg business with Marilyn and invites his new partner over for a home-cooked meal and some stimulating conversation. (Maurice: "Chardonnay? Napa Valley reserve. Cellared a case of it." Marilyn: "Fruity." Maurice: "How's your fish?" Marilyn: "Good.")

Adam's Szechwan Chicken: ("The Bumpy Road to Love," 1991) Adam walks through Joel's office door and into his life once again—this time, to bring the good doctor to his cabin to attend to his ailing wife, Eve. (Joel: "Do you realize the humiliation you caused me last year? Nobody believed me. I'm telling them, yeah, I saw Adam, Cicely's own bigfoot—Mr. Sasquatch. He cooked me pot stickers and Szechwan chicken in a wok in the middle of nowhere.")

Chicken Pot Pies: ("Slow Dance," 1991) Shelly fumes over an old female friend of Holling's who has come to visit. (Shelly: "Is anybody hungry? I could put the chicken pot pies in.")

Joel's Roast Grouse: ("A-Hunting We Will Go," 1991) Maurice, Holling, and Chris go hunting with a soon-to-be-remorseful Joel, who bags his first bird and then makes a futile attempt to save its life. (Joel: "He tastes good, kind of like an exotic chicken. . . . I've never eaten a patient before.")

Chicken-Fried Steak: ("Spring Break," 1991) As spring fever hits Cicely, Maurice falls hard for no-nonsense Officer Barbara Semanski, who's in town to investigate a mysterious rash of thefts. (Maurice: "Why don't you relax? Put your feet up? I'll make us a nice lunch. I could whip up some chicken-fried steak—potatoes au gratin." Semanski: "I'm gonna dust for prints.")

Mooseburgers: ("Pilot," 1990) In this, the first "Northern Exposure" episode, Dr. Joel Fleischman arrives in Cicely, Alaska, and meets the eccentric residents who will be calling him "neighbor" for the next four years. (Ed: "How do you like the mooseburger?" Joel: "A little gamy." Ed: "You'll get used to it.")

Ruth-Anne's Pot Roast: ("A-Hunting We Will Go," 1991) Ruth-Anne's upcoming birthday prompts Ed to panic that old age and bad habits will lead to her imminent death. (Ruth-Anne: "Me, I'm from the real meat and potatoes school. I want to eat what I want to eat. At my age I can live with a dormant sex life—but no pot roast is a sacrifice I'm not willing to make.")

The Brick's Spaghetti and Meatballs: ("Ill Wind," 1992) After Joel and Maggie take a tumble for each other in the barn, they saunter over to The Brick for a meal. (Maggie: "I'll have spaghetti." Joel: "Sounds good. Extra meatballs for me.")

Ruth-Anne's Meat Loaf: ("Blowing Bubbles," 1992) Ruth-Anne's materialistic son, Matthew, comes to town to escape the corporate jungle, and the two reminisce about his favorite meal as a child. (Ruth-Anne: "You were . . . meat loaf?" Matthew: "With the bacon and ketchup on top.")

Schmulke Bernstein's Kosher Spareribs: ("A Kodiak Moment," 1990) While Joel and Maggie preside over a birthing class in a remote Alaskan village, their thoughts turn to faraway places. (Maggie: "Where were you just now?" Joel: "Me? On the lower East Side. Eating kosher spareribs at Schmulke Bernstein's.")

Maggie's Leg of Lamb: ("Get Real," 1991) Holling's aversion to Shelly's feet, and his subsequent marriage proposal, get Shelly mad. She moves in with Maggie, who offers dinner and a less-than-inspiring soliloquy on the bliss of being single. (Maggie: "Ruth-Anne had a special on leg of lamb. I usually don't make it 'cause it's just me. But I thought with the two of us. . . . I'll rub it with garlic and rosemary—make some couscous.")

Ruth-Anne's Pork Chops: ("Blowing Bubbles," 1992) When Ruth-Anne's son Matthew comes for a visit, Ruth-Anne prepares what she thinks is his favorite meal, but it turns out that pork chops are the favorite of her *other* son, Rudy.

Shelly's Hot Dog and Cheese Casserole: ("Slow Dance," 1991) The arrival of Holling's longtime female friend prompts Shelly to worry that she and Holling don't share a common history. She attempts to remedy the situation by immersing herself in pre-1970 culture. (Shelly: "You like your martini with an olive or a twist? . . . Dinner's ready! Hot dog and cheese casserole. I made it myself.")

Black Bean Enchiladas: ("Our Tribe," 1992) As a thank-you for treating Mrs. Noanuk, a tribal elder, Joel is "adopted" into the tribe. After completing several rituals, including giving away all of his worldly possessions and fasting, Joel is christened "Heals With Tools" and given a bountiful meal. (Ed: "Mrs. Noanuk made black bean enchiladas.")

Adam's Pumpkin Tortellini: ("Roots," 1991) Adam's culinary skills are once again on display at The Brick. (Ruth-Anne: "Holling, the pumpkin tortellini is out of this world. Who's the new chef?")

Maurice's Pasta with Cayenne Tomato Sauce: ("Slow Dance," 1991) Maurice plays host to two men who are considering setting up house in Cicely and is thrilled to discover that his guests share a fondness for gourmet cooking and Broadway show tunes. His joy turns to self-doubt, however, when he learns that the men are gay. (Ron: "It's delicious . . . really good." Maurice: "I think just a tad more cayenne. . . . Chow's on. Ron, can you grab the pasta?")

6 SIDE DISHES

Chris's Glazed Carrots: ("The Big Kiss," 1991) Chris loses his voice when he sees a beautiful woman, and an old Indian spirit instructs him that only beauty can restore it.

Consequently, Chris decides to woo Maggie with handwritten notes and a home-cooked meal. (Maggie: "Glazed carrots would be fine.")

Ratatouille: ("The Bumpy Road to Love," 1991) Maurice hosts a dinner for his new love, Officer Barbara Semanski, and Holling and Shelly. (Shelly: "You'd never know this French stuff was vegetables.")

Wild Rice Stuffing: ("A-Hunting We Will Go," 1991) Eager to experience the thrill of the hunt, Joel tags along with Holling, Maurice, and Chris on a bird shoot. Excitement turns to remorse when he actually wings a grouse and his attempts to save the bird's life fail. (Ed: "How about stuffing him?" Joel: "Stuffed and mounted, staring down at me with those bright shining eyes . . . I don't think so." Ed: "I meant wild rice kind of stuffing.")

Maggie's Couscous: ("Get Real," 1991) Maggie offers to make dinner for houseguest Shelly, who's upset that Holling had led her to believe she was sterile. (Maggie: "Ruth-Anne had a special on leg of lamb. . . . I'll rub it with garlic and rosemary—make some couscous.")

Adam's Cumin Noodles: ("Aurora Borealis," 1990) Joel encounters Adam, the alleged Bigfoot of Alaska. (Joel: "You're not Adam. Adam is big, and terrifying, and wild—which granted you are—but he's not the kind of person who stirs noodles in a wok." Adam: "You know . . . I just might have to kill you to teach you a lesson. . . . Too much cumin . . . and your flame is too high.")

Marilyn's Seasoned Potatoes: ("The Bad Seed," 1992) Joel and Maggie have dinner at Marilyn's house. (Joel: "Marilyn, these potatoes are delicious. What's in them, butter? Salt? A little nutmeg maybe?" Marilyn: "Salt.")

Potatoes au Gratin: ("Spring Break," 1991) Love—and lust—are in the air as Cicely awaits the annual spring meltdown and Officer Barbara Semanski comes to town. (Maurice: "I could whip up some chicken-fried steak—potatoes au gratin.")

Lightfeather Duncan's Mashed Potatoes: ("War and Peace," 1991) Ed courts his love, Lightfeather Duncan, with letters written by Chris. (Father Duncan: "Let us give thanks for the gifts we are about to receive. Especially Lightfeather's mashed potatoes. They look great.")

7 BREADS

Maggie's Bran Muffins: ("On Your Own," 1992) Maggie finds herself becoming somewhat domesticated as a result of her attraction to Mike Monroe. (Maurice: "You don't cook." Maggie: "Oh, well, no, I don't . . . 'cook, cook.' But I bake. Yeah, I bake all the time. Muffins. You know, bran muffins. Corn muffins. A lot of muffins.")

Maggie's Corn Muffins: ("On Your Own," 1992) See above.

New York–Style Bagels: ("A Kodiak Moment," 1990) Joel is homesick for the foods of New York as he prepares to teach a birthing class in a remote Alaskan village, with Maggie as his helper. (Maggie: "You had me do a two-hour turnaround to Anchorage to pick up *bagels*? They were supposed to be medical supplies." Joel: "You know what your problem is? You don't take time to smell the bread." Maggie: "I smell the bread plenty, Fleischman, when I bake it. I don't call for five-thousand-mile take-out.")

Sage Bread: ("A-Hunting We Will Go," 1991) While Joel mourns his failed attempt to save the life of the grouse he shot, Ed has more practical ideas about the bird. (Ed: "Baked, with sage bread and chestnuts. It'd make a real feed.")

Rye Currant Rolls: ("Oy Wilderness," 1991) Maggie and Joel are stranded in the wilds of Alaska when their plane malfunctions. (Maggie: "I used to want to be a chef. . . . Yeah. Well, a baker, actually. Not desserts. Just bread. Really good bread. Baguettes, little rye currant rolls like the ones at the Poulaine Bakery on the Rue de la Cherche Midi.")

Banana Bread à la Maggie: ("On Your Own," 1992) Maggie takes on an uncharacteristic nurturing personality as her feelings toward Mike Monroe deepen. (Ruth-Anne: "She cooked?" Mike: "She baked all morning. Kelp loaf. Banana bread.")

8 DESSERTS

Banana Cream Pie: ("The Russian Flu," 1990) "Northern Exposure" pays tongue-in-cheek homage to "Twin Peaks" when Holling takes Joel and his fiancée, Elaine, out for some scenic viewing. (Holling: "Y'all want some hot coffee or doughnuts?" Joel: "You wouldn't happen to have some cherry pie?" Holling: "No, but I got some banana cream. . . .")

Lemon Meringue Pie: ("Spring Break," 1991) As Cicely awaits the annual spring meltdown, Holling is itching for a fight with anyone who'll take him on. (Restaurant patron: "The lemon meringue was good today.")

Holling's Special Lime Chiffon Pie: ("Things Become Extinct," 1992) Ed searches for a "vanishing breed"—or something that is becoming extinct—to film. (Ed: "I need something really rare. Somebody who can make something nobody else can make, or do something nobody else can do. Like those pies of Holling's." Shelly: "The lime chiffon with the crushed pineapple?" Ed: "And the graham cracker crust." Shelly: "He got that recipe from the back of a box of Jell-O.")

Zabaglione: ("The Bumpy Road to Love," 1991) When Joel is summoned to Adam's cabin to attend to Eve's ailments, he literally becomes a hostage to her hypochondria and to the couple's endless bickering. (Eve: "Did he tell you how we met? It was a book party. I was in publicity, an editor—corner office at Knopf . . . And there was Adam—the caterer—this dark, brooding man in a chef's hat. We went back to his place. He whipped up some zabaglione—I've been with him ever since.")

Ruth-Anne's Chewy Oatmeal Cookies: ("What I Did for Love," 1991) Joel plans a trip home to New York, but Maggie's dreams of his death in a plane crash—as well as Cicely's enthusiasm for his temporary replacement, Dr. Dave Ginsburg—make him reconsider his vacation plans. (Ruth-Anne: "I should hit the road, too. Just dropped by for a sec to give Dave some of the cookies I baked." Ginsburg: "Oatmeal. My favorite." Joel: "You baked him cookies?")

Maggie's Fudge: ("On Your Own," 1992) Maggie's attraction to Mike Monroe grows, and her uncharacteristic behavior, including wearing pretty dresses and cooking from scratch, surprises the townsfolk. (Ruth-Anne: "She did make fudge once.")

Ruth-Anne's Birthday Carrot Cake: ("A-Hunting We Will Go," 1991) While Joel, Holling, Maurice, and Chris go grouse hunting, Ed organizes a surprise birthday party for Ruth-Anne. (Holling: "You did a nice job on the cake, hon." Shelly: "And you on the tweet-tweets.")

9 THANKSGIVING

("Thanksgiving," 1992) Joel discovers that he owes the state of Alaska yet another year of service, and the town celebrates Thanksgiving, known as the Day of the Dead to the native Indians, with a bountiful feast, a festive parade, and the traditional tossing of tomatoes at white people.

Taco Salad with Fresh Guacamole: Maggie and Shelly plan the Thanksgiving menu. (Shelly: "Don't forget the taco salad." Maggie: "With fresh guacamole.")

Roast Turkey with Giblet Gravy: Mike Monroe decides to risk the wrath of his faulty immune system by eating something besides kelp loaf. (Mike:"I know I'm going to pay for this, but what the hell. Pass me a drumstick and some of those candied yams.")

Mike's Eggplant Parmesan: Mike Monroe offers up his organic vegetable crop for the Thanksgiving feast. (Mike: "I've got bushels of Japanese eggplants—you know, the little ones? And, uh, I was thinking, maybe you'd like to come over. You and I could whip up another dish for the feast. Eggplant parmesan.")

Candied Yams: Hyperallergic Mike Monroe risks death-by-sweet-potato at the town's Thanksgiving meal. (Mike: "Pass me a drumstick and some of those candied yams.")

Plantains: Maggie and Shelly's Thanksgiving menu includes some rather nontraditional dishes. (Maggie: "What else? Last year's list was twice as long. Tortillas, plantains, lentils . . .")

Baked Lentils: See above.

Saffron Rice: Mike Monroe surprises Maggie by venturing out of his protective bubble to attend the Thanksgiving feast. (Maggie: "I wish I knew you were coming—I would've made something special. Maybe this rice. . . . I don't know about the saffron. What do you think?")

Risotto: This is included on Maggie and Shelly's eclectic Thanksgiving menu. (Maggie: "Potatoes au gratin . . . risotto . . .")

Cranberry-Walnut Relish: This is also on the menu. (Shelly: "Cranberry sauce?" Maggie: "Cranberry sauce! How could I forget that? And walnuts.")

Day of the Dead Sugar Cookies: Some of Cicely's residents pay tribute to the traditional Indian Day of the Dead celebration by baking these. (Shelly: "Don't forget to bring your skull-and-crossbones cookie cutter to the big baking tonight." Ruth-Anne: "All right. And I thought we could make some sugar cookies in the shape of gravestones." Shelly: "Neat-o.")

Chris's Pumpkin Pie: Chris reminisces about the best Thanksgiving he ever had, which was during his incarceration. (Chris: ". . . the mellow sweetness of pumpkin pie off that metal tanginess of a prison spoon is something you will never forget. . . .")

10 CHRISTMAS IN CICELY

("Seoul Mates," 1991) As the Christmas season arrives, Maurice is visited by a woman from his past and the half-Korean son he never knew he had, Maggie gets a surprise when her parents decide to spend the holidays in the Caribbean without her, Shelly yearns for the traditional Catholic celebrations she grew up with, and Joel tries to cope with his affection for Christmas customs and his own Jewish heritage.

Ruth-Anne's Raven Bread: The townsfolk pay homage to the Indian legend of the Raven as they prepare for the Christmas holidays. (Ruth-Anne: "Raven bread. I make it every Christmas. Try some." Joel: "Mmm. Pumpernickel. I'll take a loaf.")

Dave's Eggnog: Maggie and Shelly are preoccupied with their own thoughts of Christmases past. (Shelly: "Dave made eggnog." Maggie: "Eggnog—wonderful! You know, I'm really looking forward to Christmas Eve. . . . It'll be quiet, peaceful. . . ." Shelly: "Holy.")

Old-Fashioned Plum Pudding with Hard Sauce: Nothing could be more indicative of Christmas to Joel than this dish. Try as he might, he can't bring himself to thoroughly embrace the trappings of the season. (Joel: "Scratch the plum pudding—there's a matzo ball underneath. I'm a Jew—that's all there is to it.")

Joel's Oven-Roasted Chestnuts: Joel attempts to join in the Christmas spirit. (Joel: "I've got some chestnuts. I can put them in the oven.")

Matzo Ball Soup: See Old-Fashioned Plum Pudding with Hard Sauce.

11 A RUSSIAN FEAST

("War and Peace," 1991) When the Russian entertainer Nikolai Ivanovich Appolanov makes his annual visit to Cicely, all are overjoyed to see their old friend again—all except Maurice, who carries a patriotic grudge against the musician's homeland.

The Brick's Borscht: The town prepares to celebrate Nikolai's return. (Chris: "That's right, our old friend Nikolai Appolanov, months early and not a moment too soon. So cook up your best borscht, and resin those bows. For my part, I'll commence continuation of our annual reading of *War and Peace* . . . soon as I can find the book.")

Pirozhki: These delicacies are served at the party held for Nikolai. (Nikolai: "Have a pirozhaki." Joel: "Thanks.")

Roast Chicken: Also served at the party.

Russian Pot Roast: Also served at the party.

Kasha: Also served at the party.

Boiled Potatoes: Also served at the party.

12 POTLUCK FARE

Monk's Cassoulet: ("Revelations," 1992) When Chris secludes himself in a monastery, he is shocked to discover that he has sexual feelings for one of the monks (who turns out to be a woman). He's also a bit surprised that the monastic life includes such gourmet cuisine as cassoulet.

Green Bean Casserole: ("Family Feud," 1992) Maggie and Mike Monroe prepare this dish for the celebration following the unveiling of Marilyn's clan's totem pole.

Maggie's Lasagna: ("Spring Break," 1991) The townsfolk hold a potluck dinner to celebrate the annual spring ice melt. (Shelly: "What'd you bring?" Maggie: "Lasagna." Shelly: "Mmm, yummy. I made lasagna, too. So'd Ruth-Anne. So'd Gary. So'd Chris.")

Ruth-Anne's Lasagna: (see above)

Shelly's Lasagna: (see above)

Joel's Jell-O Supreme: ("Spring Break," 1991) Joel contributes to the spring potluck. (Joel: "Hey, people like Jell-O. Besides, it's the only alternative to lasagna out there. What'd you make?" Maggie: "Tuna casserole.")

☞ INDEX ☜